At Issue

The Ethics of Cloning

Other Books in the At Issue Series:

At Issue

| The Ethics of Cloning

David M. Haugen, Susan Musser and Kacy Lovelace,
Book Editors

GREENHAVEN PRESS
A part of Gale, Cengage Learning

GALE
CENGAGE Learning·

Detroit • New York • San Francisco • New Haven, Conn • Waterville, Maine • London

GALE
CENGAGE Learning™

Christine Nasso, *Publisher*
Elizabeth Des Chenes, *Managing Editor*

© 2009 Greenhaven Press, a part of Gale, Cengage Learning.

Gale and Greenhaven Press are registered trademarks used herein under license.

For more information, contact:
Greenhaven Press
27500 Drake Rd.
Farmington Hills, MI 48331-3535
Or you can visit our Internet site at gale.cengage.com

For product information and technology assistance, contact us at

Gale Customer Support, 1-800-877-4253
For permission to use material from this text or product, submit all requests online at
www.cengage.com/permissions

Further permissions questions can be emailed to permissionrequest@cengage.com

Articles in Greenhaven Press anthologies are often edited for length to meet page requirements. In addition, original titles of these works are changed to clearly present the main thesis and to explicitly indicate the author's opinion. Every effort is made to ensure that Greenhaven Press accurately reflects the original intent of the authors. Every effort has been made to trace the owners of copyrighted material.

Cover photograph © Images.com/Corbis.

LIBRARY OF CONGRESS CATALOGING-IN-PUBLICATION DATA

The ethics of cloning / David M. Haugen, Susan Musser and Kacy Lovelace, book editors.
    p. cm. -- (At issue)
    Includes bibliographical references and index.
    ISBN 978-0-7377-4312-8 (hardcover)
    ISBN 978-0-7377-4311-1 (pbk.)
    1. Cloning--Moral and ethical aspects--Popular works. I. Haugen, David M., 1969- II. Musser, Susan. III. Lovelace, Kacy
    QH442.2.E846 2009
    176--dc22
                                                        2008054001

Printed in the United States of America
1 2 3 4 5 6 7 13 12 11 10 09

Contents

Introduction

In 2004 Hwang Woo Suk, a biomedical scientist and professor from South Korea, stunned the medical world by announcing that his research team—which had previously been working on cloning livestock—had cloned a human embryo. This feat, which most scientists had considered impossible because of the complex nature of primate biology, was made more remarkable when Hwang's team further claimed that it had successfully extracted stem cells from the embryo. Within months of this astounding accomplishment, Hwang reported in 2005 that his continued experiments had made gathering stem cells seem almost easy. He told the magazine *Science*—which had also covered his 2004 breakthrough—that he had gleaned eleven embryonic stem cells from 185 eggs donated by women of various ages, a high rate of success for something that had so long eluded scientists working in primate cloning.

In late 2005, however, scandal about the possibility that the women research subjects were coerced into donating their eggs forced Hwang to resign from many of the posts he held. And in December of that year, his work was forever tarnished when Seoul National University revealed to the world that Hwang's stem cell achievements had been faked. The promised breakthrough had not come, and what advocates of human cloning had hoped for seemed now mired not only in ethical questions about the feasibility of this science but also in the moral dubiousness of its research practices.

Writing in the *National Review* Online, Robert George and Eric Cohen maintained that cloning supporters would try to "spin" Hwang's problem of exploiting women donors into a need to legalize stem cell research in the United States, where "it would proceed under stricter ethical supervision." But both George, a professor of jurisprudence, and Cohen, a fellow of the Ethics and Public Policy Center, argue that this manipulation of the facts would not hold up under scrutiny. They assert that respectable physicians would never invite women donors to undergo the risky and demanding egg-extraction process for a controversial and unproven science. Furthermore, George and Cohen state that "no decent society would countenance the buying and selling of human eggs on the open market." The authors go on to make the weightier claim against cloning for stem cells by insisting that a human embryo "is an individual human life in its earliest stage," and the death of such individuals for the harvesting of stem cells disrespects the value of human life.

Katrien Devolder and Julian Savulescu, a pair of ethics professors whose viewpoints are contained within *At Issue: The Ethics of Cloning*, counter some of the arguments against embryonic stem cell research by insisting that stem cells can be taken from discarded embryos created during in vitro fertilization treatments. And, while not dismissing the "humanness" that some people impart to these embryos, Devolder and Savulescu believe that society has an ethical obligation to eradicate diseases and genetic disorders by unlocking the therapeutic secrets of embryonic stem cells. They warn, "Through a failure of moral imagination we may continue to hold back cloning research and be responsible for the deaths of many people who perished while we delayed the development of treatments."

While Devolder and Savulescu saw Hwang's research (before it was shown to be fraudulent) as pointing the way toward further embryonic stem cell research, George and Cohen contend that "the South Korea scandal only strengthens the case for developing scientific alternatives to research cloning." For many, the use of adult stem cells—those taken from adult tissues, not nascent embryos—is an obvious way out of the ethical problem of destroying potential life. In addition, medical treatments using adult stem cells have already been successful whereas the use of embryos in therapeutic cloning is still of unproven value.

In addition, critics such as Wolfgang Lillge, a doctor and editor, propose that if condoned, the methods involved in therapeutic cloning will be used to move beyond mere therapy. As Lillge argues, "no one can escape the fact that, should one wish to use embryonic stem cells for 'therapeutic purposes,' the very techniques will be developed that will also be used for the cloning of human beings, the making of human-animal hybrids, the manipulation of germ lines, and the like." Such fears may make some Americans oppose therapeutic cloning on ethical grounds, but select nationwide polls suggest that a slight majority favors stem cell research. A 2005 poll by the Coalition for the Advancement of Medical Research, for example, found that 59 percent of Americans would unhesitatingly support embryonic stem cell research—a result that climbed to 68 percent when the proposed benefits of this research were explained. The vast majority, however, still disapprove of human cloning.

It is uncertain whether human cloning or therapeutic cloning using embryonic stem cells will ever gain enough support to change current prohibitory laws in the United States. But America does not hold a monopoly on bioscience, nor does it dictate global morality. For this reason, many observers believe the progress of cloning may be unstoppable. And while concerns about the value of human life and the process of creation will always haunt this science, researchers will continue to set their own ethical limits, and some, like Hwang Woo Suk, will endeavor to push the possibilities to an end that may be unconscionable to some but miraculous to others. *At Issue: The Ethics of Cloning* offers a variety of perspectives on the controversial science of cloning and the ethical guidelines that will help shape its course. While some of these viewpoints concern the morality of conducting cloning research, others take for granted the allegedly unstoppable nature of this research and look ahead to the ethical questions that will preoccupy a world in which cloning is commonplace.

1

The Ethics of Cloning: An Overview

Aaron D. Levine

An assistant professor in the School of Public Policy at Georgia Tech, Aaron D. Levine writes about the ways in which ethics debates influence ongoing research in emerging biotechnology fields. Specifically, he has assessed the impact of government policies on embryonic stem cell research worldwide. Levine is the author of Cloning: A Beginner's Guide *and editor of* States and Stem Cells: The Policy and Economic Implications of State-Funded Stem Cell Research.

The science of cloning will almost inevitably shape human existence as we know it from this point forward. With cloning for food and therapeutic purposes being pursued with some level of success and the cloning of humans looming on the horizon, it is important that individuals participate in informed debate about the ethical implications of this technology. Comprehending the science of cloning is essential to understanding how cloning will shape the future, and this understanding will aid everyone in weighing the potential costs and benefits of this groundbreaking technology.

Cloning technology was invented during the twentieth century and now is poised to help define the twenty-first. Almost everyone has heard of Dolly, the cloned sheep born in 1996 but what about the rapid progress made since then? Scientists now count horses, cows, cats, and dogs among the

Aaron D. Levine, *Cloning: A Beginner's Guide.* Oxford, U.K.: OneWorld, 2007. Copyright © Aaron D. Levine 2007. Reproduced by permission.

many animals they can clone. This progress raises a host of questions. Are you comfortable drinking milk or eating meat from a cloned cow? Should we clone extinct or endangered species? Will the April 2005 birth of Snuppy, the world's first cloned dog, usher in a new era of cloned pets? Should we clone embryos to generate embryonic stem cells and help develop medical therapies? And perhaps the most important question of all: when, if ever, will this progress lead to the first cloned human?

Creating an Informed Debate

Although scientists are nearly unified in their opposition to cloning humans for reproductive purposes, on-going research toward other goals makes this likely, if not inevitable. For the most part, this research is driven by the hope that cloning technology will have significant health benefits, perhaps leading to transplantation therapies that use embryonic stem cells specifically tailored to individual patients. Of course, if a cloned human is ever born, the desire for fame will almost certainly play a role. Looking back to the media frenzy surrounding the birth of the first test tube baby in 1978 or the clamor surrounding the birth of Dolly, it is not hard to imagine the furor that a cloned human baby would generate.

By and large, cloning is not what you see in the movies.

As modern biotechnology is increasingly applied to humans, it raises important questions for society to address. Should we, perhaps in the relatively near future, allow infertile couples or single mothers to use cloning technology to try to produce a child? Should we, in the longer term, permit parents to use cloning technology not just to have children, but to have children with specific genetic modifications or enhancements? Debates on cloning technology and its implications are, all too often, hijacked by advocates or opponents who skew the science to fit a particular view. Although the details of cloning research are complex, the general technique is not particularly difficult to understand. And understanding this general technique and its consequences is more than enough to participate fully in these important debates and to see through the many myths clouding discussions of cloning.

The Science of Cloning

Cloning is, at its most basic level, reproduction without sex. "Sex" does not refer to the act of intercourse but to sexual reproduction—the joining of genetic material from two parents into an embryo that may, if development goes well, give rise to a new adult organism. All humans alive today were born through sexual reproduction; a single sperm from the male joined with an egg from the female, creating an embryo with half its genetic material derived from each parent. This mixing of genetic material introduces an element of chance into reproduction, ensuring that children differ genetically from their parents. In cloning, offspring are genetically identical to their single parent. Such offspring are the products of "asexual" reproduction.

Cloning, rather than relying on the merging of egg and sperm, uses the genetic material or DNA from a single cell. This cell is joined to an egg from which the DNA has been removed. Next, this construct is coaxed to develop as if it were a newly fertilized egg. If development proceeds normally, the resulting organism will be genetically identical to the single donor. In this case, reproduction no longer generates new combinations of genetic material but faithfully duplicates previously existing ones.

Although mammals do not normally reproduce asexually, nature does provide a close analogy: identical twins. Roughly one out of every 250 human births results in identical twins— siblings that are genetically identical. Because a cloned child would be genetically identical to its DNA donor, it can be helpful to imagine cloning as a form of delayed twinning. If cloning technology were perfected and applied to humans, the birth of a cloned human would not be altogether unlike the birth of identical twins but instead of a few minutes separating the two births, there could be many years.

Scientists speculate that a cloned human and his or her parent would typically be less similar than identical twins. This is because the environment plays an important role in development. Identical twins usually share much of the same environment, while a cloned human and his or her genetic parent often would not. Identical twins develop in the same uterus and usually grow up in the same household. In contrast, a cloned human would probably be carried in a different womb and grow up in a different household from its genetic parent. The cloned child would also be born into a world that had changed significantly. The importance of environmental influences has led bioethicists who have considered the possibility of human cloning to focus on its unpredictability. It is not clear that a child cloned from Mozart or Pavarotti would grow up to perform or even appreciate music.

Human vs. Animal Cloning

Humans have not been cloned and few plausible reasons exist to clone humans for reproductive purposes. Some have suggested that cloning might provide a means for infertile parents to have a genetically related child. However, fertility research seems likely to lead to other, more effective and less controversial, approaches to treat the few couples for whom this last resort might be necessary. Others have suggested cloning may be justified when a child dies young; believing parents would deserve a chance to bring their lost loved one back to life. But many think this would lead to disappointment all round. Due to environmental influences, the cloned child would not be the same as the deceased child he or she was ostensibly replacing. Furthermore, the new child, forever competing against an idealized memory, might face unreasonable expectations. In the end, neither parents nor child would prosper.

Cloning matters because it is on the verge of affecting daily life around the world and its importance will only grow with time.

Because human cloning seems remote and is generally undesired, cloning science today focuses primarily on animal research. In animals bred for human use, such as cows, pigs, and horses, the advantages of asexual reproduction are significant. The element of chance central to sexual reproduction frustrates animal breeders and livestock producers. When mating a prize-winning stud to promising mare, horse breeders aren't excited by the chance that the resulting foal will randomly receive the parents' worst genes: they want to propagate the genes that turned the stud into a champion, in the hope of producing future winners. Cloning, by allowing breeders to produce genetic replicas of valuable animals, makes this process more efficient. For horse racing, this efficiency comes at a steep price, as cloned horses are currently forbidden from participating in officially sanctioned races. These sorts of restrictions don't apply to pigs or cows, which are bred to produce meat and milk for consumers, rather than for competition. Not surprisingly, livestock breeders, particularly in the United States, have shown interest in using this technology to make their operations more productive and more profitable.

Hollywood Cloning Myths

By and large, cloning is not what you see in the movies. It is not photocopying; or at best it is like using a slow and blurry photocopier—so slow, that by the time the copy is made, the original has changed. If you cloned your dog today, there wouldn't be an exact replica running around and barking tomorrow, as suggested in the Arnold Schwarzenegger hit *The Sixth Day*. Rather, you would create an embryo that could potentially be transferred into the womb of a surrogate mother. Nine weeks later, if all went well, a puppy would be born. This puppy would be genetically identical to your dog but, obviously, much younger. It might look like its parent had looked as a puppy but it would experience a different environment and, perhaps, mature differently.

Movies such as *Multiplicity*, in which an overworked contractor clones himself to help cope with his busy life, ignore the time delay essential to cloning. In this case, the movie's premise, while entertaining, is absolutely wrong. The clones, rather than helping out at work and around the house, would be a burden. They would be infants, not adults as portrayed in the movie, and like any human infants would need nearly constant attention. As any parent can tell you, adding a baby (or several) to your family is not a good strategy for gaining extra time.

Nor does cloning bring back the long-dead. Cloning technology, at least at its current efficiency levels, requires a significant amount of biological material. For living animals, it is simple to take a sample and preserve this material: Dolly, for instance, was cloned from frozen cells. However, finding enough genetic material presents a significant hurdle to cloning long-extinct species. For now, the cloning of dinosaurs, as seen in *Jurassic Park* and its successors, is no more than a scientific pipe dream. That said, scientists have made progress in cloning endangered species and some believe cloning may offer a promising conservation strategy. Attempts to clone recently extinct animals, such as the Tasmanian tiger, where preserved biological material may still exist, remain a possibility.

As we shall see, cloning is not easy. When Dolly was born, she was the only success in 277 attempts. Success rates have improved but the procedure remains inefficient. Many cloned embryos fail to develop, and when development does start, a variety of abnormalities are seen. Even in the most efficient operations, only a minority of the original cloned embryos develop to term and go on to lead healthy lives. At the moment, this inefficiency limits the usefulness of animal cloning for commercial purposes. It also raises the ire of animal rights activists, who complain that the technology produces deformed animals. Obviously, these inefficiencies would need to be overcome before scientists could even begin to consider cloning humans for reproductive purposes.

Cloned Animals for Food

Cloning matters because it is on the verge of affecting daily life around the world and its importance will only grow with time. Animal cloning will revolutionize food production in the coming years and may, by turning animals into biological factories, revolutionize pharmaceutical production as well. Moving from animals to humans, cloning technology may, if some expectations prove true, radically alter medicine, leading the way to an era of personalized transplant therapies. Finally, in the longer term, it opens the door to the cloning (and potential genetic engineering) of humans, perhaps changing the very essence of what it means to be a human being.

A growing scientific consensus suggests that milk and meat from cloned animals, or at least from their progeny, are safe for human consumption. In December 2006, the U.S. Food and Drug Administration announced preliminary plans to allow products from cloned livestock into the food supply. If finalized, such a ruling could have dramatic effects. Scientists can clone several important farm animals, including cows and pigs, but only a small number of cloned animals—none destined for consumption—live on American farms today. One industry insider has estimated that within twenty months of a ruling allowing products from cloned animals into the food supply, American farms would be covered with hundreds of thousands of clones. This could occur despite widespread consumer discomfort with the very idea of eating products from cloned animals.

Thus far, the United Kingdom and most other European countries have shown more caution regarding the introduction of cloned animal products into the food supply. If, as appears likely, the United States approves these products first, it could contribute to continued trade wars. Although cloning does not necessarily include genetic modification, some cloned products will almost certainly also be genetically modified. Thus, trade in cloned products could get tangled in the ongoing debate on the import of genetically modified organisms; a number of countries have limited their imports of agricultural products from nations where genetic modification is prevalent.

When Dolly was cloned in 1996, the research was primarily funded by a biotechnology firm that aimed to revolutionize the way drugs are produced. . . . The basic idea is to create, through cloning, genetically modified sheep or cows that produce therapeutic compounds, such as insulin or growth hormone, in their milk. Pharmaceutical companies could isolate these valuable compounds from the milk for a fraction of the cost of traditional manufacturing methods. The milk would not be intended for human consumption and would probably be discarded after the therapeutics had been isolated. This technique, known as "pharming," offers potential economic benefits for drug companies and has taken off since Dolly's birth. Numerous cows have been bred to produce therapeutics in their milk and some scientists are exploring the possibility of harvesting drugs from other body fluids, including urine. Pharming raises a number of concerns, including the risk of drug-producing animals accidentally entering the food supply. Although the risks may be remote, even those of us unfazed by drinking milk from a cloned cow wouldn't be pleased to find out the milk was significantly enriched with a prescription medicine.

The Future of Cloning

While cloned animals that produce therapeutic compounds already exist, the creation of cloned human embryos to facilitate medical therapies remains in the future and raises serious ethical questions. Many scientists are optimistic that cloning will, one day, regularly be used to create stem cells genetically matched to specific patients. These cells could, potentially, help treat a range of debilitating conditions, such as type 1 diabetes and Parkinson's disease. Because the cells would be genetically matched to the individual patient, they might avoid the immune rejection problems that complicate transplant therapies today. This potential therapeutic technique is controversial, however, because deriving these patient-matched stem cells, using currently envisioned approaches, would require the creation of a cloned human embryo. At five days of age, the stem cells would be isolated from the embryo and the developmental process halted. Dramatic advances toward this vision of regenerative medicine were reported by a group of researchers based in South Korea, but in late 2005 the veracity of this work was called into question: today, it is clear that most, if not all, these advances were fraudulent. Despite this set-back, many scientists believe the vision remains promising and "therapeutic cloning" is being pursued by scientists around the world.

Cloning also matters because, given the field's current trajectory, it is part of our shared future. From the food supply to the medicine cabinet, cloning technology is poised to change the way we live. But these changes are controversial. Each of us can and should participate in the debates that will shape the role cloning plays in the future. Before you say "yuck" to drinking milk from cloned cows or rush off to save your dog's DNA in preparation for eventual cloning, take the time to learn a bit about the science. Although cloning is fairly simple, misinformation is prevalent. Understanding the science behind cloning will help make these debates more meaningful and their outcomes more satisfactory for everyone.

2

Human Cloning Should Be Banned

Leon R. Kass

Leon R. Kass served as chairman of the President's Council on Bioethics from 2001 to 2005, where he and his colleagues addressed issues such as cloning, stem cell research, genetic technologies, and the general philosophical and ethical impacts of biomedical advances on society. He received a PhD in biochemistry from Harvard in 1967 and is the author of books such as The Ethics of Human Cloning *(coauthored with James Q. Wilson) and* Life, Liberty, and the Defense of Dignity: The Challenge for Bioethics. *Leon R. Kass is currently a fellow at the American Enterprise Institute and the Harding Professor of Social Thought at the University of Chicago.*

While no scientist has successfully cloned a human to date, the possibility that the world will soon see its first human clone looms on the horizon. Many advanced countries worldwide have banned research that could lead to human cloning; however, all attempts to legislate such a ban in the United States have thus far failed. This failure is due in large part to the way in which the issues of human cloning and stem cell research have become closely, but wrongly, intertwined. Now, scientific advances have rendered the cloning of human embryos for scientific research unnecessary because new and more efficient ways of obtaining or creating embryonic stem cells have been discovered. Thus the United States has reached a point where human cloning can be

Leon R. Kass, "Defending Life and Dignity: How, Finally, to Ban Human Cloning," *Weekly Standard*, vol. 13, February 25, 2008. Copyright © 2008, News Corporation, Weekly Standard. All rights reserved. Reproduced by permission.

banned and human dignity can be preserved without sacrificing the ability to conduct potentially life-saving research.

In his [January 2008] State of the Union address President [George W.] Bush spoke briefly on matters of life and science. He stated his intention to expand funding for new possibilities in medical research, to take full advantage of recent breakthroughs in stem cell research that provide pluripotent stem cells without destroying nascent human life. At the same time, he continued, "we must also ensure that all life is treated with the dignity that it deserves. And so I call on Congress to pass legislation that bans unethical practices such as the buying, selling, patenting, or cloning of human life."

As in his previous State of the Union addresses, the president's call for a ban on human cloning was greeted by considerable applause from both sides of the aisle. But Congress has so far failed to pass any anti-cloning legislation, and unless a new approach is adopted, it will almost certainly fail again.

Past Failures to Ban Human Cloning

Fortunately, new developments in stem cell research suggest a route to effective and sensible anti-cloning legislation, exactly at a time when novel success in cloning human embryos makes such legislation urgent. Until now, the cloning debate has been hopelessly entangled with the stem cell debate, where the friends and the enemies of embryonic stem cell research have managed to produce a legislative stalemate on cloning. The new scientific findings make it feasible to disentangle these matters and thus to forge a successful legislative strategy. To see how this can work, we need first to review the past attempts and the reasons they failed.

Three important values, differently weighted by the contending sides, were (and are) at issue in the debates about cloning and embryonic stem cells: scientific and medical progress, the sanctity of human life, and human dignity. We seek to cure disease and relieve suffering through vigorous research, conducted within acceptable moral boundaries. We seek to protect vulnerable human life against destruction and exploitation. We seek to defend human procreation against degrading reproductive practices—such as cloning or embryo fusing—that would deny children their due descent from one father and one mother and their right not to be "manufactured."

Embryonic stem cell research pits the first value against the second. Many upholders of the sanctity of human life regard embryo destruction as unethical even if medical good may come of it; many partisans of medical research, denying to nascent human life the same respect they give to life after birth, regard cures for disease as morally imperative even if moral harm may come of it. But the deepest challenge posed by cloning has to do not with saving life or avoiding death, but with human dignity, and the cloning issue is therefore only accidentally bound up with the battle about stem cell research. Yet both parties to the stem cell debate happily turned the cloning controversy into the life controversy.

The Entangling of Stem Cell Research and Cloning

The faction favoring embryonic stem cell research wanted to clone embryos for biomedical research, and touted cloning's potential to produce individualized (that is, rejection-proof) stem cells that might eventually be used for therapy. Its proposed anti-cloning legislation (the Kennedy-Feinstein-Hatch bill) would ban only "reproductive cloning" (cloning to produce children) while endorsing the creation of cloned human embryos for research. Such cloning-for-biomedical-research its proponents originally called "therapeutic cloning," hoping that the goal of "therapy" would get people to overcome their repugnance for "cloning." But when that strategy backfired, they disingenuously denied that the cloning of embryos for research is really cloning (they now call it, after the technique used to clone, SCNT, somatic cell nuclear transfer). They also denied that the product is a human embryo. These Orwellian [propagandistic] tactics succeeded in confusing many legislators and the larger public.

The age of human cloning is here, and the first clones, alas, do not read "made in China."

The faction opposed to embryonic stem cell research wanted to safeguard nascent human life. Its proposed anti-cloning legislation (the Weldon-Stupak bill in the House, the Brownback-Landrieu bill in the Senate) would ban *all* human cloning—both for reproduction and for biomedical research—by banning the initial step, the creation of cloned human embryos. (This is the approach I have favored, largely because I thought it the most effective way to prevent the production of cloned children.) But most of the bill's pro-life supporters cared much more that embryos not be created and sacrificed than that children not be clones. Accordingly, they sought to exploit the public's known opposition to cloning babies to gain a beachhead against creating embryos for destructive research, which practice, although ineligible for federal funding, has never been illegal in the United States. Initially, this strategy worked: In the summer of 2001, the Weldon-Stupak bill passed the House by a large bipartisan majority. (It has been passed again several times since.) But momentum was lost in the Senate, owing to delays caused by 9/11 [2001 terrorist attacks] and strong lobbying by the pro–stem cell forces, after which time an impasse was reached, neither side being able to gain enough votes to close debate.

A Mediating Voice on Bioethics

Concerned that the United States appeared to be incapable of erecting any moral barriers to the march toward a Brave New World, the President's Council on Bioethics (I was then its chairman) sought to show the president and Congress a way forward. Setting aside our deep divisions (on the moral status of human embryos and federal funding of stem cell research), we successfully sought common ground and recommendations on which we could all agree.

In our 2004 report, *Reproduction and Responsibility*, we unanimously proposed a series of legislative bans to defend human procreation against certain egregious practices—practices that would blur the boundary between the human and the animal, exploit the bodies of women, deny children the right to normal biological lineage, and commodify nascent human life. We called for legislative moratoria on: the placement of a human embryo in the body of an animal; the fertilization of a human egg by animal sperm (or vice versa); the transfer of a human embryo to a woman's uterus for purposes other than producing a child; the buying, selling, and patenting of human embryos or fetuses; and (on the cloning front) the conception of a child other than by the union of egg and sperm, both taken from adults—a provision that would ban cloning as well as other unwelcome forms of reproduction.

Though these recommendations received a favorable response from the White House and from some members of Congress (in both parties), our recommendations were attacked from both sides. The scientists and the assisted-reproduction professionals, as anticipated, wanted no restrictive federal legislation whatsoever. Surprisingly, we were hit also from the right: Several leading pro-lifers objected to the "children's provision" on the ground that it appeared to be a retreat from the Brownback total ban on cloning—a bill they nevertheless conceded had no chance of passage in the Senate. To my astonishment, some powerful lobbyists privately told me they objected also to the animal-transfer provision, on the grounds that one should not ban any method that might rescue "extra" IVF [in vitro fertilization] embryos that would otherwise die [because in order to ensure a woman becomes pregnant many embryos are fertilized and frozen, but once a child is conceived, the remaining embryos go unused]. (When pressed on this point, one interlocutor said that she would gladly give a child a pig for a mother if that were the only way to rescue an otherwise doomed embryo!)

Of the Council's sensible recommendations, only one has been enacted: a ban on initiating a pregnancy for any purpose other than to produce a child. (This bill, enacted as an anti-"fetal-farming" rather than a defense of women measure, also amended the existing statute to forbid the use of cells or tissues derived from a human embryo gestated in an animal.)

Scientific Advances Negate the Need for Therapeutic Cloning

Fast forward to [February] 2008. We are in the last year of the Bush presidency. Despite the president's numerous calls for action, we remain the only major nation in the high-tech world that cannot summon itself to ban human cloning, thanks to the standoff over the embryo issues. Fortunately, science has given Congress another chance to act. In the last six months, the scientific landscape has changed dramatically. On the one hand, the need for anti-cloning legislation is now greater than ever; on the other hand, there are reasons why a new approach can succeed.

Here is what's new. After the 2005 Korean reports of the cloning of human embryos turned out to be a fraud, many said that human cloning could not be achieved. Yet late in 2007 Oregon scientists succeeded for the first time in cloning primate embryos and growing them to the blastocyst (5–7-day) stage, and then deriving embryonic stem cells from them. More recently, other American scientists, using the Oregon technique, have reported the creation of cloned human embryos. The age of human cloning is here, and the first clones, alas, do not read "made in China."

On the stem cell front, the news is decidedly better. In the last two years, several laboratories have devised methods of obtaining pluripotent human stem cells (the functional equivalent of embryonic stem cells) without the need to destroy embryos. The most remarkable and most promising of these approaches was reported last November [2007] by both Japanese and American scientists (including Jamie Thompson, the discoverer of human embryonic stem cells). It is the formation of human (induced) pluripotent stem cells (iPSCs) by means of the reprogramming (also called de-differentiation) of somatic cells. Mature, specialized skin cells have been induced to revert to the pluripotent condition of their originating progenitor.

The therapeutic usefulness of this approach has also been newly demonstrated, by the successful treatment of sickle cell anemia in mice. Some iPSCs were derived from skin cells of an afflicted mouse; the sickle cell genetic defect in these iPSCs was corrected; the treated iPSCs were converted into blood-forming stem cells; and the now-normal blood-forming stem cells were transferred back into the afflicted mouse, curing the disease.

Pro-lifers and scientists can come together to ban these practices in America, as they have already been banned in the rest of the civilized world.

Scientists have hailed these results. All parties to the stem cell debates have noted that the embryonic-stem-cell war may soon be over, inasmuch as science has found a morally unproblematic way to obtain the desired pluripotent cells. But few people have seen the implications of these developments for the cloning debate: Cloning for the purpose of biomedical research has lost its chief scientific *raison d'être* [reason for being]. Reprogramming of adult cells provides personalized, rejection-proof stem cells of known genetic make-up, directly from adults, and more efficiently than would cloning. No need for human eggs, no need to create and destroy cloned embryos, no need for the inefficient process of deriving stem cell colonies from cloned blastocysts. Ian Wilmut himself, the British scientist who cloned Dolly the sheep, has abandoned his research on cloning human embryos to work with reprogrammed adult cells.

Another effect of this breakthrough is that the value for stem cell research of the spare embryos that have accumulated in IVF clinics has diminished considerably, defusing the issue of the ban on federal funding of such research. Why work to derive new stem cell lines from frozen embryos (of unknown quality and unknown genetic composition, and with limited therapeutic potential owing to transplant immunity issues) when one can work with iPSCs to perfect the reprogramming approach and avoid all these difficulties?

Legislation Everyone Can Agree On

That's not the only way the new scientific landscape changes the policy and legislative pictures. We are now able to disentangle and independently advance all three of the goods we care about. First, it now makes great sense to beef up federal support for regenerative medicine, prominently featuring ramped-up work with iPSCs (and other non-embryo-destroying sources of pluripotent human stem cells). The timing is perfect. The promise is great. The potential medical payoff is enormous. And the force of example for future public policy is clear: If we exercise both our scientific wit and our moral judgment, we can make biomedical progress, within moral boundaries, in ways that all citizens can happily support.

Second, we should call for a legislative ban on all attempts to conceive a child save by the union of egg and sperm (both taken from adults). This would ban human cloning to produce children, but also other egregious forms of baby making that would deny children a link to two biological parents, one male and one female, both adults. This approach differs from both the Kennedy-Feinstein-Hatch and the Brownback-Landrieu bills, yet it could—and should—gain support from people previously on both sides. It pointedly neither endorses nor restricts creating cloned embryos for research: Cloning embryos for research is no longer of such interest to scientists; therefore, it is also no longer, as a practical matter, so important to the pro-life cause. Moreover, the prohibited deed, operationally, should be the very act of *creating* the conceptus (with intent to transfer it to a woman for pregnancy), not, as the Kennedy-Feinstein-Hatch bill would have it, the *transfer* of the proscribed conceptus to the woman, a ban that would have made it a federal offense *not* to destroy the newly created cloned human embryos. The ban proposed here thus deserves the support of all, regardless of their position on embryo research.

Third, the time is also ripe for a separate bill to defend nascent life, by setting up a reasonable boundary in the realm of embryo research. We should call for a (four- or five-year) moratorium on all *de novo* [Latin for "from the beginning," "afresh," or "anew," here refering to creation of new embryos] creation—by whatever means—of human embryos for use in research. This would block the creation of embryos for research not only by cloning (or SCNT), the goal of the Brownback-Landrieu anti-cloning bill, but also by IVF. Such a prohibition can now be defended on practical as well as moral grounds. Many human embryonic stem cell lines exist and are being used in research; 21 such lines, still viable, are available for federally funded research, while an even greater number are being studied using private funds. The new iPSC research, however, suggests that our society can medically afford, at least for the time being, to put aside further creation of new human life merely to serve as a natural resource and research tool. We can now prudently shift the burden of proof to those who say such exploitative and destructive practices are absolutely necessary to seek cures for disease, and we can require more than vague promises and strident claims as grounds for overturning the moratorium.

Time to Join the Civilized World

Morally and strategically speaking, this triple-pronged approach has much to recommend it. It is at once more principled, more ambitious, and more likely to succeed than its predecessors. By addressing separately the cloning and embryo-research issues, we can fight each battle exactly on the principle involved: defense of human procreation or defense of human life. By broadening the first ban to include more than cloning, we can erect a barrier against all practices that would deny children born with the aid of reproductive technologies the ties enjoyed by children conceived naturally. By extending the second ban to cover all creation of life solely as an experimental tool, we can protect more than merely embryos created by cloning. We would force everyone to vote on the clear principles involved: Legislators would have to vote yea or nay on both weird forms of baby-making and the creation of human life solely for research, without bamboozling anyone with terminological sleights of hand. And by combining these legislative restrictions with strong funding initiatives for regenerative medicine, we can show the American people and the world that it is possible to vigorously pursue the cures we all dearly want without sacrificing the humanity we rightly cherish.

Politically as well, this triple-pronged approach is a winner for all sides. Because the latest science has made creating embryos for research unnecessary and inefficient by comparison with reprogramming, we have the chance to put stem cell science on a footing that all citizens can endorse. Indeed, in return for accepting a moratorium on a scientific approach that is not very useful (creation of new embryos for research), scientists could exact large sums in public support for an exciting area of science. With pro-lifers as their biggest allies, they could obtain the research dollars they need—and their supposed enemies would write the biggest checks. Meanwhile, at the very time the latest science has made affronts to human procreation—cloning, but not only cloning—more likely and even imminent, pro-lifers and scientists can come together to ban these practices in America, as they have already been banned in the rest of the civilized world, without implicating the research debate at all.

In an election year [2008], Congress will be little moved to act quickly on these seemingly low priority items. Moreover, the partisans who have produced the current impasse may still prefer to keep things at stalemate, the better to rally their constituents against the other side. But we can ill afford to be complacent. The science is moving very rapidly. Before the end of the summer, we may well hear of the cloning of primate babies or perhaps even of a human child. Now is the time for action, before it is too late.

Human Cloning Should Not Be Banned

Kerry Lynn Macintosh

Kerry Lynn Macintosh is a professor of law at Santa Clara University in California. Topics of her writings include electronic commerce, commercial law, and contracts; additionally, she has researched the relationship between the law and biotechnologies such as assisted reproduction, cloning, and genetic engineering. She is the author of Illegal Beings: Human Clones and the Law.

Legislating a federal ban on human cloning would have grave consequences not only for the individuals who engage in cloning and are born as a result of this technology, but also for society as a whole. Enacting a ban on human cloning would infringe on the freedom of individuals to reproduce and have genetically related offspring and would also reduce scientific freedom in the United States. Even if a ban on human cloning became law, children would still be born as a result of clandestine cloning. History suggests that these cloned children would face discrimination, as a result of the ban, not unlike that experienced by African Americans prior to the Civil Rights movement. Further, this type of ban would undermine the very egalitarian principles upon which the government of the United States is based, making it bad public policy.

Antimiscegenation laws [which outlawed interracial marriage in the United States until 1967] were bad public policy. Their costs outweighed their putative benefits.

Kerry Lynn Macintosh, *Illegal Beings: Human Clones and the Law*. New York: Cambridge University Press, 2005. Copyright © Kerry Lynn Macintosh 2005. Reprinted with the permission of Cambridge University Press.

The laws injured the men and women who were denied the fundamental right of marriage. The laws also injured the children of mixed-race couples by subjecting them to existential segregation and stigmatizing them as inferior. In addition, the laws denied mixed-race children legitimacy and the legal and social benefits of that status.

The legislatures that enacted antimiscegenation laws, and the courts that upheld them, disregarded these costs in favor of flimsy and speculative "evidence" regarding the supposed degeneracy and inferiority of mixed-race unions and children. This evidence included scientific studies purporting to establish that blacks are physically and mentally inferior to whites and that racial mixing leads to children who are inferior.

Today, most people recognize and acknowledge that antimiscegenation laws were bad public policy. Unfortunately, they have not recognized or acknowledged that laws against human reproductive cloning are bad public policy. Policymakers and lawmakers have emphasized the putative benefits of these laws and minimized or ignored their costs.

> Marriage and procreation are fundamental to the very existence and survival of the race. The power to sterilize, if exercised, may have subtle, far-reaching and devastating effects. . . . There is no redemption for the individual whom the law touches. Any experiment which the State conducts is to his irreparable injury. He is forever deprived of a basic liberty.

In this [viewpoint], I seek to reverse this trend and provide a fresh public policy analysis of laws against human reproductive cloning. The [viewpoint] first identifies the costs that such laws impose—not only upon existing adults *but also upon the innocent children who will be born through cloning technology.*

Unfortunately, policymakers and lawmakers have virtually ignored the costs that anticloning laws will impose on human clones. . . .

Violating Procreative Freedom

If human reproductive cloning is banned in the United States, men and women who cannot reproduce safely or effectively via sexual reproduction will lose the chance to have children who are genetically related to them. This is more than a personal loss. The U.S. Supreme Court has recognized a constitutional right to privacy that includes reproductive freedom. This freedom includes the right to procreate through cloning when that is the only option.

A brief history will help to explain this conclusion. In 1942, in the landmark case of *Skinner v. Oklahoma*, the Supreme Court first identified procreation as a fundamental right deserving of special protection. In that case, the Court invalidated an Oklahoma law that mandated sterilization of certain criminals but not others who had committed offenses of comparable seriousness. The Court held that the law violated the Equal Protection Clause of the Fourteenth Amendment. The Court subjected the law and its meaningless distinctions among crimes and criminals to strict scrutiny because procreation was at stake.

A growing number of attorneys and legal scholars have argued that reproductive freedom should include the right to employ cloning.

Constitutional scholars have identified this case as the beginning of the development of the constitutional right of privacy (even though the *Skinner* court never used that particular term of legal art). The reader is probably more familiar with cases like *Griswold v. Connecticut*, which recognized that the right to privacy includes the right of married couples to use contraception, or *Roe v. Wade* and its progeny, which recognized the right of a woman to have an abortion up to the point of fetal viability. Recent cases such as these have focused on the right of fertile men and women *not* to reproduce because laws threatened that right. Since *Skinner*, there have been few cases that directly addressed the right to procreate largely because the government has very seldom interfered with that right in recent years. In vitro fertilization (IVF) was never outlawed despite the public outcry over "test-tube babies" when it was a new technology. For the most part, the government has left infertile men and women free to pursue their medical treatments without interference.

For a man who has no functional sperm or a woman who has no functional eggs, sexual reproduction is not possible even with the benefit of IVF. If reproductive cloning develops to the point at which it is safe and effective, it could provide many infertile men and women with the only means possible of having genetically related offspring.

On the basis of this reality and cases like *Skinner* and *Lifchez*, a growing number of attorneys and legal scholars have argued that reproductive freedom should include the right to employ cloning—at least for infertile men and women who cannot reproduce sexually. The same argument could be made on behalf of carriers of heritable diseases for whom sexual reproduction is too hazardous. Arguably, the liberty to clone should also be granted to gays and lesbians, who can have genetic children through sexual reproduction but only if they accept gametes from persons who are not their sexual partners.

Any law that infringes on the fundamental right to reproduce is subject to strict scrutiny. In other words, the government must prove a compelling interest in support of the law and show that it is narrowly drawn to vindicate that interest. In a fair fight, the government would not be able to make this case for anticloning laws. . . .

Granting Greater Freedom to Some Citizens

Of course, few fights are fair. The Supreme Court might hesitate to recognize a right to clone for political reasons. The

Court has taken much abuse over the years for extending the privacy right to include abortion. It might be reluctant to issue another opinion that could be as controversial as *Roe v. Wade.*

What if the Supreme Court refuses to hold that the right to privacy includes a right to clone? If no right to clone exists, how could a national ban injure reproductive freedom?

The answer is simple. The right to privacy is not stated expressly in the U.S. Constitution. Some of its applications, notably the right to an abortion, are unpopular with the public and many legislators. Once the Supreme Court starts to chip away at reproductive freedom, further erosions become more likely.

Professor John Charles Kunich has made an intriguing argument along these lines. In his view, a "moderate" law that permits research cloning but bans reproductive cloning could serve as a Trojan Horse to overturn *Roe v. Wade.* Such a law would require researchers to destroy cloned embryos; any attempt to give them life by implanting them in a womb would be a crime. When confronted with such a repugnant "clone then kill" law, the Supreme Court might be motivated to rethink the entire question of whether nascent human life deserves protection against destruction. If it does, the right to abortion logically must come into question.

The costs of a national ban, moreover, would not be limited to the erosion of reproductive freedom as such. If the Supreme Court holds that there is no right to clone, even for those who cannot reproduce by other means, the Constitution will stand for the proposition that men and women who are fertile, healthy, and heterosexual enjoy greater procreative freedom than men and women who are infertile, disabled, or homosexual. This antiegalitarian outcome would devalue the humanity of infertile, disabled, and homosexual men and women. Further, among these victims, such unjust treatment would breed contempt for the Constitution itself. These, too, should be counted among the costs of a national ban on cloning.

Infringement on Scientific Freedom

A national ban on human reproductive cloning could infringe not only on reproductive freedom but on scientific freedom as well.

To date, the U.S. Supreme Court has not held that there is a constitutional right to conduct scientific research. Legal scholars, however, have attempted to locate protection for scientific research under the First Amendment. Some contend that, if the First Amendment protects the dissemination of scientific information, it also must protect the scientific research that creates the information. Otherwise, the government could control ideas by choking them off at the source. Others argue that scientists who experiment are like protesters who burn flags; their conduct is symbolic speech that merits First Amendment protection.

Whenever scientific experimentation is limited, we forfeit not just knowledge but also all the useful technologies that could have been derived from that knowledge.

Although a complete analysis is beyond the scope of this [viewpoint], it is interesting to think about how these theories might apply to human reproductive cloning. For example, the research necessary to perfect human reproductive cloning, including clinical trials that insert cloned embryos into the wombs of willing participants, may be protected as a precondition to the publication of scientific information regarding human reproductive cloning. A flat ban on human reproductive cloning can be characterized as a content-based restriction on knowledge. As such, the law would violate the First Amendment unless it was the least restrictive means of achieving a compelling interest. However, . . . most objections to cloning are weak rather than compelling. Even safety concerns will wane over time as scientists involved in animal and research cloning continue to advance our knowledge and technical proficiency. Moreover, a flat ban goes further than necessary to protect children and other participants in cloning and can be challenged on the ground that it is not the least restrictive means of ensuring safety.

Alternatively, reproductive cloning might be protected as symbolic speech. For example, one author has argued that the act of cloning expresses the idea that there should be no limits on science. Any law designed to stop scientists from "playing God" relates to this idea and could be an unconstitutional attempt to suppress symbolic speech. The act of cloning also challenges prevailing views of human individuality. Any law that banned cloning to protect such views would be an unconstitutional attempt to suppress symbolic speech.

The government might claim that it wants to ban cloning for reasons unrelated to the suppression of speech. A national ban could pass constitutional muster if these governmental interests were important and the incidental restriction on symbolic speech was no greater than essential to further those interest. Again, however, most of the five objections to cloning are weak, and safety concerns will dwindle over time.

Although the foregoing arguments show some promise, their success is not guaranteed. Given the lack of precedent protecting scientific research, it is hard to predict how the Supreme Court would react if confronted with the claim that there is a First Amendment right to engage in reproductive cloning. The public and media are likely to view any scientist who wants to clone as a crank or worse. The Court might be reluctant to champion such an unpopular person or cause and could uphold a national ban on reproductive cloning.

To many readers, this might not seem like a significant loss. Few mainstream scientists or doctors are interested in pursing human reproductive cloning. However, a case about reproductive cloning could have a broader impact because it would force the Supreme Court to address the question of whether the First Amendment protects scientific research and, if so, to what extent. To justify upholding a ban on reproductive cloning, the Court might adopt a narrow view of the First Amendment and its protections for scientific experimentation. If this occurs, the ban on reproductive cloning will have damaged scientific freedom more generally. Ultimately, this would hurt not just scientists but also the rest of society; whenever scientific experimentation is limited, we forfeit not just knowledge but also all the useful technologies that could have been derived from that knowledge.

Reproductive Cloning, Despite the Laws

On the assumption it can survive constitutional challenges brought under the right to privacy or the First Amendment, a national ban on human reproductive cloning is likely to be somewhat effective. The criminal and civil penalties are so extreme that many people will be deterred from using the technology to have children. As a result, many perfectly normal babies will not be born. This is the core goal of existential segregation, of course, but it has costs—not only for families who lose valuable members but also for society, which loses the many physical, intellectual, and emotional contributions that the babies would have made throughout their lives.

However, a national ban on cloning will not be entirely effective.... I have identified three groups that may have an interest in reproductive cloning: infertile men and women who lack viable gametes, carriers of heritable diseases, and gays and lesbians. In addition to the powerful urge to reproduce, these individuals may feel contempt for the laws that have discriminated against them and see no reason to obey the laws so long as detection and punishment can be avoided.

This raises the question of how these individuals might gain access to cloning services. Fertility doctors are not likely to offer reproductive cloning in defiance of a legal ban and its penalties. They can make plenty of money from legal technologies like IVF (which can be offered together with donor eggs or sperm to patients who lack viable gametes). "The fact remains, however, that there are thousands of fertility doctors, technicians, clinics, and laboratories in the United States with the expertise and equipment required to harvest eggs, perform nuclear transfer (using micromanipulation equipment that is a standard feature in many laboratories), cultivate embryos, and transfer them to the womb. Some people who want to have a child through cloning will belong to this group of professionals or have spouses, relatives, or friends who do, and thus will have access to the expertise and equipment necessary to do it themselves."

Another possible scenario is that research scientists could be fooled by "patients" who pay them to clone embryos ostensibly to obtain stem cell therapies but in fact to obtain embryos that can be used for reproductive purposes. Scientists engaged in research cloning will have the eggs, equipment, and expertise to create healthy embryos. Once created, the "patients" could transfer the embryos to fertility clinics, lie about the origins of the embryos, and have them transferred to the womb.

Finally, American citizens who want to reproduce asexually might flock to offshore fertility clinics and come home with cloned pregnancies or babies.

In short, if human reproductive cloning is possible, and safe enough to attract clients, many babies will be born through cloning no matter what the law says. Thus, I proceed to consider the costs that a national ban would inflict on human clones. . . .

The Stigma of Restrictive Legislation

Social psychologists define a "stigma" as a sign or mark that designates the bearer as defective and less valuable than "normal" people. Categories of stigmatizing conditions include tribal identities (e.g., race, religion, or nation), blemishes of individual character (e.g., mental disorders or a criminal conviction), and abominations of the body (e.g., physical deformities or disease). In addition to marking those who bear them as less worthy than others, stigmas often evoke social identity through the device of stereotypes regarding people who share the same stigma.

Human clones bear the stigma of the "duplicative" genomes that they share with other humans who existed before them. This genetic stigma is not visible but is potent nevertheless. If the stigma is revealed, it links the bearer to all of the harmful stereotypes about "clones". . . .

A baby born in defiance of the national ban [on cloning] would be marked as unworthy of existence.

Moreover, social psychologists have shown that individuals who bear a stigma are more likely to experience derision, exclusion, discrimination, and even violence at the hands of nonstigmatized persons. Victims of discrimination can lose jobs, housing, insurance, and other resources; victims of social exclusion can lose friends and romantic partners. Aware of their own devalued identities, many stigmatized individuals experience stress and a loss of self-esteem. This research strongly implies that human clones are also likely to face discrimination, stress, and psychological damage on account of the genetic stigma they bear.

Anticloning laws will take this bad situation and make it much worse.

To understand why, consider the historical root of the term "stigma." In ancient Greek society, criminals and traitors were cut with knives and burned with branding irons. The resulting mark, or "stigma," served as a potent symbol of their immorality and unworthiness. A person bearing a stigma was considered unfit for normal society.

Today, laws can serve the same function as knives and branding irons. Laws are a powerful statement of what the majority of the people in a society believe and what is right and just. Laws can mark a certain class of human being as immoral or unworthy, thereby justifying others in abusing or discriminating against them. . . .

The Supreme Court has recognized that legal stigma can do serious harm. In the landmark case of *Brown v. Board of Education*, the Court invalidated laws that segregated blacks from whites in public schools. The key to the Court's ruling was its recognition that the laws imposed a stigma: "To separate [children] from others of similar age and qualifications solely because of their race generates a feeling of inferiority as to their status in the community that may affect their hearts and minds in a way unlikely ever to be undone." Reasoning that separate was inherently unequal, the Court held that the segregation laws violated the equal protection guarantee.

Sodomy laws provide another example of the damage that legal stigma can do. In general, these laws prohibited oral or anal sex, or both—even between consenting adults. In the United States, the majority of the laws applied to heterosexual sex as well as homosexual sex. Most people, however, perceived the laws as prohibitions on homosexual sex. The laws sent the message that gays and lesbians are criminals. This, in turn, caused gays and lesbians to suffer psychological damage; anxiety and self-loathing were the predictable consequences of such categorization. Worse, the message that gays and lesbians are criminals was taken as a signal that they were entitled to less than equal treatment in the workplace and home. Bigots used the laws to justify employment and housing discrimination. The laws also encouraged vigilantes to commit violence against gays and lesbians as a kind of informal enforcement mechanism. In 2003, the Supreme Court finally eliminated this particular legal stigma by ruling that sodomy laws violate the constitutional right to privacy.

Legislating Discrimination

Let us return to reproductive cloning and the legal stigma that a national ban would impose on human clones. Any time conception, implantation, or gestation took place within the United States in violation of the ban, the resulting baby would, by definition, be someone whom lawmakers did not want to exist. The same would be true of any baby born after parents "imported" a cloned embryo or fetus into the United States; if the import ban had worked, the parents would not have traveled abroad for cloning services, and the baby would not exist.

Thus, a baby born in defiance of the national ban would be marked as unworthy of existence. Moreover, to the extent a national ban would be based on the five objections, it would be based on the many stereotypes about human clones that underlie those objections. Thus, the ban would also incorporate and validate the stereotypes, presenting them as the *reasons* why human clones are unworthy of existence.

For example, on the basis of the opinions expressed in policymaking reports and Congressional debates, if Congress ever bans cloning, it will be, in part, due to the identity fallacy. Thus, a national ban would mark human clones as unworthy of existence *because they are copies*. The ban would validate not only this root stereotype but also all of the stereotypes that logically flow from it. It would mark human clones as evil, unoriginal, fraudulent, inferior, zombielike, constrained, pathetic, disturbed, disgusting, identity thieves, destroyers, a threat to democratic values, and subhuman. . . .

Reasoning by analogy to the experience of gays and lesbians with sodomy laws, we can see that the legal stigma of a national ban on cloning would have devastating consequences for human clones. By making human clones as unworthy of existence, the ban would damage their self-esteem and cause psychological damage. Also, by making human clones as unworthy of existence, the ban would send the message that they are not entitled to the equal treatment that humans ordinarily enjoy under the law. This would embolden bigots who already do not like human clones to perpetrate employment and housing discrimination. Finally, and most dangerously, any law that marks human clones as unworthy of existence would encourage vigilantes to kill them as a kind of informal enforcement mechanism. . . .

Overcoming Prejudice Against Clones

Much has been made of the threat that human clones and their recycled lives supposedly pose to autonomy and democratic society. But too few have remarked on the threat that anticloning laws and their ugly message of inequality pose to egalitarianism. It would be ironic indeed if America managed to overcome its historical legacy of slavery and racism only to embrace a new form of discrimination marking some humans as less valuable than others based on their shared genomes.

> *A national ban on cloning would establish a new category of legally stigmatized humans; in so doing, it would undermine our society's commitment to egalitarian principles.*

Each and every time the law draws invidious distinctions between classes of humans, the basic principle of egalitarianism is undermined no matter how few people are affected. Each and every successful attack on the principle of egalitarianism invites further attacks as the government becomes emboldened to search out other unpopular groups and discriminate against them also.

Optimists might insist that a vital factor tends to safeguard egalitarianism despite such attacks: our common humanity.

Stereotypes can be hard to change; yet, they are vulnerable to experience. When people come into personal contact with members of a stigmatized group, they start to accumulate data that indicate the stereotypes could be untrue. Enough data may cause them to rethink and reject stereotypes. Alternatively, simply bringing stigmatized individuals within a group can, by redefining boundaries between "us" and "them," give the nonstigmatized members of the group a strong psychological incentive to abandon the disparaging stereotypes they once held.

Thus, for example, if we could get to know human clones at school, on dates, or in the workplace, we could develop enough facts to learn the truth. Contrary to the claims of their opponents, we would not find them to be unnatural, manufactured, copied, or deformed freaks. Also, if circumstances required us to include them openly in our classrooms, work groups, and other social organizations, we would have a strong incentive to recognize their humanity.

However, a national ban on cloning would deprive us of that opportunity. By reducing births and driving those who are born underground or into the closet, the ban would make it harder for us to gain experience with human clones. We would have fewer chances to learn that stereotypes about them are untrue and that we share a common humanity with the members of this supposedly subhuman class.

It might be argued that, even in the absence of personal contact, media accounts of human clones could help to dispel such false images. However, . . . the media has not been friendly to cloning. For every story that tells the truth about cloning, there are many others that misstate or exaggerate the facts in a manner calculated to titillate the public and sell more television advertisements, newspapers, or magazines.

Given this history, the media cannot be counted upon to set the record straight. Even if the media reforms itself and tries to tell the truth, many people very sensibly will not trust what they see on television or read in the papers until they experience it for themselves.

Undermining Egalitarian Principles

Meanwhile, a national ban on cloning would take on a life of its own. By eliminating or greatly reducing personal experience with human clones, the laws would make it much harder for us to recognize that the arguments that inspired the laws were based on false stereotypes. In this way, the laws would tend to protect themselves against repeal. Moreover, opponents of cloning would be sure to assert that the very existence of the laws justified their premises and continued existence, further stacking the odds against repeal.

In sum, a national ban on cloning would establish a new category of legally stigmatized humans; in so doing, it would undermine our society's commitment to egalitarian principles. This problem would be unlikely to correct itself. The national ban would drive unpopular and unwanted human clones underground or into the closet, making it hard for the rest of us to learn the stereotypes about them to be untrue. This, in turn, would make it harder to reject the stereotypes. Ignorance would perpetuate the ban and its antiegalitarian influence.

4

Human Cloning Will Be Accepted When It Is Safe and Effective

Joe Leigh Simpson

Joe Leigh Simpson is the executive associate dean of academic affairs at Florida International University. Prior to taking this position, he was a professor in the Department of Obstetrics and Gynecology and the Department of Molecular and Human Genetics at Baylor University. Simpson has written extensively on reproductive genetics and the societal impact of biotechnological advances.

Public acceptance of new technologies is often closely related to the safety and efficacy of these technologies. After any technology is shown to reliably produce positive results for humanity as a whole, society begins to become more tolerant of its use. Such is also the case with both therapeutic and reproductive cloning. As therapeutic cloning has advanced, more people have supported the continuation of research to fully explore its applicability in treating and curing diseases. Likewise, if reproductive cloning were shown to be safe, the majority of people would begin to accept it as a form of reproductive aid for those who are unable to have their own biological children, and this sentiment would eventually outweigh that of others who would remain opposed to the technology.

Joe Leigh Simpson, "Could Cloning Become Permissible?" *Reproductive BioMedicine Online*, vol. 14, supplement. 1, pp. 125–129, 2007. Copyright © 2007 Reproductive Healthcare Ltd. Reproduced by permission.

Strong opinions exist as to whether either therapeutic cloning or reproductive cloning is necessary. Of course, strong opinions are expected whenever new technologies are pursued, especially if biological or medical in nature. These opinions are reasoned initially on mostly ethical grounds, a process that tends to yield all or none responses. Thus, reproductive cloning is universally condemned. Less monolithic is the response to therapeutic cloning (embryonic stem cells/somatic cell nuclear transfer). Here there are dichotomous responses: a panacea for intractable disease requiring regenerative therapy or a totally unacceptable option because current technology requires damage to or loss of a potentially viable embryo. Depending on jurisdiction and source of funding, therapeutic cloning does or does not proceed.

Yet decisions about incorporating new technology do not proceed so simply. Many technologies that at first seemed arguable become well accepted. Why the change? Presumably factors other than a purely ethical analysis must play pivotal roles in societal acceptance. Perhaps society's initial ethical analysis of such controversial scientific advances is inchoate, with greater understanding and clarity awaited, pending further scientific advances. The purpose of this contribution is to consider from the perspective of a physician and reproductive geneticist whether therapeutic or reproductive cloning is necessary.

Problems of Either–Or Ethics

Conventional treatises concerning therapeutic cloning inevitably focus around one's definition of abortion. If the blastocyst from which embryonic stem cells (ESC) must be derived is defined as a person, therapeutic cloning is not ethically considered acceptable irrespective of how salutary ESC might prove to be for regenerative medicine. Of course, others do not agree that the blastocyst is a person. They reason instead that a blastocyst should be treated with respect, but does not deserve the same protection as a live-born baby. If this general belief is accepted, a secondary decision then becomes necessary. Should a blastocyst be utilized only if from a spare embryo, destined to remain cryopreserved or discarded? Or can any embryo be used, including those created for the express purpose of its inner cell mass being used to produce ESC for therapeutic cloning? [Philosophy professor Bonnie] Steinbock reasons that there is no substantive distinction between using 'spare embryos' and utilizing embryos created for an explicit purpose.

If scientific success, e.g. improving the clinical management of intractable disease or injury with therapy having an acceptable risk seems imminent, resistance tends to dissipate.

To date, ethical reasoning about cloning has proceeded by asking 'either–or' questions that are also *a priori*, i.e. not informed by scientific and clinical experience. Is an embryo a person with rights that rule out cloning of any kind, or is an embryo simply to be treated with respect that allows therapeutic cloning? Can one use only spare embryos or is provenance irrelevant? Such an 'either–or,' *a priori*, approach invites binary, unnuanced, absolute responses. However, the public and much of the scientific community insert an element of pragmatism into what is misleadingly treated as a set of *a priori* 'either–or' choices. This is especially true for physicians, who tend to be highly pragmatic. They ask 'Is success a reasonable likelihood?' Are there more than two, 'either–or' alternatives? These kinds of questions shift reasoning away from an 'either–or,' *a priori*, approach to a more pragmatic, scientifically and clinically informed approach.

Liberal and Conservative Orthodoxy

The initial response of the public and the scientific community to new technology is usually resistance. Adherence to the *status quo* (orthodoxy) is the typical reflex. This arises from both political conservatives as well as political liberals. Conservatives tend to espouse the *status quo, per se.* Sometimes this is based on religious tenets. Liberals decry the lack of egalitarianism they believe new technologies may bring. They reason that if expensive medical advances cannot be offered to the entire population, none should benefit. Not infrequently, this belief merges with idealism, for example wondering whether the dollars saved by not pursuing new technologies could be reapplied to longstanding healthcare needs. Overall, the result is paralysis that leads to failure to pursue new technologies. A favourite endgame is proposing a moratorium to allow study, which then actually is never completed or acted on. The ineluctable outcome is that any who advocate new technologies face opprobrium disgrace from both the right as well as the left.

By decrying reproductive cloning the public unwittingly finds it more difficult to accept therapeutic cloning.

Why do so many in the scientific community go along with orthodoxy? Probably because scientists are vulnerable. They depend upon public support. They work in institutions that must answer to the public. They fear that pursuing the wrong type of research might result in their being ostracized. This has consequences that go beyond those created by mere differences of opinions. Generating laboratory funds may become insurmountable. The risk is simply too great for scientists in positions of vulnerability.

Pragmatic Medical Responses

Physicians have political biases as well as the public, but also take into account therapeutic benefits. If scientific success, e.g. improving the clinical management of intractable disease or injury with therapy having an acceptable risk seems imminent, resistance tends to dissipate. This especially becomes true if alternatives do not provide effective clinical management. Witness acceptance of heart transplants, or more recently the initial acceptance of face transplants after the first surgery was performed. Here the pivotal issue was absence of alternatives. Similarly, embryonic stem cell/somatic cell nuclear transfer is tantalizing, despite lack of noticeable human success, because it often seems to be the only plausible option for many diseases, injuries, and conditions that might, for the first time, be effectively managed by the new tools of regenerative medicine. Thus, acceptability of cloning to treat incurable disease is over 70% in a recent Greek survey of 1020 men and women.

Requirement for success prior to medical application becomes a more weighty consideration if effective alternatives already exist. Thus, deriving an ESC to produce haemopoetic stem cells seems less necessary because an alternative exists in umbilical stem cell cord blood. Similarly, reproductive cloning seems unnecessary given the obvious alternatives of conventional assisted reproduction.

Physicians are not the only ones who discipline ethical analysis by pragmatic considerations; much of the public does as well. Thus, those who now oppose ESC research, ostensibly because the embryo seems not to be treated with sufficient respect, may change their mind if shown success. That is, the innate reflex of orthodoxy is made without consideration of all consequences and, hence, may not be immutable. If reflex orthodoxy had been based solely on well constructed, *a priori* ethical reasoning, public opinion would remain uninfluenced by therapeutic success.

That the public's initial opposition to new technologies is ephemeral is legend. Opposition to prenatal genetic diagnosis predictably arose after amniocentesis was introduced, and similar arguments against were revisited decades later with preimplantation genetic diagnosis (PGD). Once these techniques were shown to be safe and accurate, public fears dissipated. IVF [in vitro fertilization] was initially widely condemned, not only in ecclesiastical circles but in the scientific community. Once success was clear, public acceptance ensued.

Resistance followed by acceptance seems a recurrent pattern. Recent examples include PGD to select human leukocyte antigen-matched embryos for transfer. Following initial ambivalence, success effectively ended the debate. The same occurred when PGD was first applied for adult onset genetic disease, especially neoplastic disorders. It was stated that PGD should be restricted to genetic disorders of childhood onset that were characterized by mental retardation; however, this argument was soon abandoned once the utility of PGD for neoplastic disease became evident.

Opposition to Therapeutic Cloning Will Dissipate

At present, society continues to debate unresolvable dichotomous ethical beliefs concerning therapeutic cloning that requires embryonic stem cells/somatic cell nuclear transfer (ESC/SCNT). However, society still awaits medical (pragmatic) benefit. If ESC/SCNT technology were to become successful, it is predicted that opposition will rapidly dissipate. This would then recapitulate the sequence when IVF was introduced in the 1970s and 1980s. Of course, there will always be those who believe that neither ECS/SCNT or IVF should ever be pursued. However, they will represent an increasing minority if ECS/SCNT is successful. Their rights to dissent by declining to participate should be accepted; however, forbidding ESC/SCNT as a matter of public policy that will affect everyone will not be the practice in most jurisdictions. The current attraction of bone marrow transplantation and pancreatic islet cell transfer to derive stem cell clones will have simply presaged this.

Stifling the Debate on Reproductive Cloning

Reproductive cloning is almost not a topic for polite scientific discussion. It is universally proscribed. Efficacy is unproved.

Safety is doubted, based upon animal data. Society also seems offended by the concept, perhaps on grounds of sensationalism (e.g. the movie *The Boys from Brazil* [in which a Nazi doctor attempts to clone Hitler following the Second World War]). Given the above, it is hardly a surprise that dialogue has not taken place. We thus remain in the stage of orthodoxy. . . .

Avoiding dialogue is unfortunate and has unintended consequences. One unintended consequence is that by decrying reproductive cloning the public unwittingly finds it more difficult to accept therapeutic cloning. As desirous as the latter is to the scientific community it may seem specious to argue that therapeutic 'cloning' is good but reproductive 'cloning' is not. Renaming therapeutic cloning by applying a new appellation (e.g. SCNT) may come across to the public as disingenuous. Thus, refusal even to discuss reproductive cloning may be adversely affecting the public debate on therapeutic cloning. That is, the public does not readily distinguish between the two types of cloning or their different purposes. Naturally, politicians follow the public; thus, acceptance is impeded not only in reproductive cloning but also in therapeutic cloning.

Whether cloning is necessary will eventually be decided not strictly on a priori *ethical grounds, but also on pragmatic medical ethics.*

Irrespective, orthodoxy reigns with discussion of reproductive cloning off limits, except for condemnation. Opprobrium is heaped upon those who suggest a need for scientific dialogue, to say nothing of experiments to determine feasibility. The scientific community uncharacteristically foregoes even academic discussion. A call is made for scientific journals not to publish on reproductive cloning. This comes even from scientists who have achieved success in animals, now professing amazement that anyone would wish to replicate the principle in humans. Scientific societies declare that no abstracts on human reproductive cloning will be accepted at their scientific meetings. Academic freedom evanesces.

Current proscriptions against reproductive cloning are indeed now appropriate on grounds of safety and lack of efficacy. However, could societal attitudes change? For example, what if reproductive cloning proved more efficient than traditional assisted reproduction? What if pregnancy success rate was higher than with conventional assisted reproduction? What if the technology proved less expensive, and safer? Under such circumstances, we have argued that the public's response to reproductive cloning might not be so immutable. Indeed, the public might already be more flexible than scientists. A 2002 Gallup Poll conducted for the Genetics and Public Policy Centre reported that 76% of the public agreed with the statement that reproductive cloning should not be pursued. However, a quarter of respondents did not hold this position. In fact, 26% of men explicitly accepted reproductive cloning, an openness especially evident among young males. In a survey of 1020 Greek men and women, 'human cloning' to treat 'reproductive problems' was considered 'probably' acceptable by 21.8% and acceptable by 10.7%. It is unclear from this survey if the respondents distinguished between reproductive cloning and therapeutic (ESC/SCNT) cloning. Irrespective, a substantial portion of the public might accept reproductive cloning if it proved efficacious. . . .

Overcoming Ethical Objections

If safety and efficacy of reproductive cloning were not a concern, would it not become obligatory to discuss ethical issues in an equitable fashion? Exceptionally, [professor of human values and ethics Carson] Strong did so at the 2005 meeting of this group [Reproductive Biomedicine Online]. The reader is referred to his thoughtful analysis. [Philosopher Dieter] Birnbacher also pointed out that many arguments espoused against reproductive cloning lack robustness, although he still reasoned that reproductive cloning should not be pursued because the process violates the concept of naturalness, transgressing a bright line. More typically, others have concluded that reproductive cloning should be proscribed for various *a priori* ethical reasons, any of which should not be circumvented. Let us consider some of these arguments.

One argument—lack of autonomy—states that even if a cloned child has autonomy in the internal sense, he/she could be subject to moulding by others in ways different from that to which non-cloned children would be subjected. Yet there is in fact little realistic fear that a cloned child would behave any differently than a conventionally conceived child. All parents have expectations for their offspring: educational, athletic, professional, personal. These are not necessarily met, no matter how directive a parent might be. It would of course, be imperative to assure that unwitting persuasion not be exerted, but in my opinion this fear can and would be obviated.

A second argument—deontology—is that each child must be unique. If not unique, a child is presumed not able to be treated with sufficient respect. However, natural examples already exist in which not every child is genetically unique. Witness monozygotic (MZ) twins. Each member of an MZ pair has identical DNA, barring somatic mutation; however, parents of MZ twins still value each individual child. Similarly, parents who undergo the rigours necessary for reproductive cloning would have already demonstrated the high value they place on obtaining a child. It is doubtful that such a child would suffer any more, or less, than a twin or any other child generally.

Scientifically, the issue of genetic uniqueness is actually moot because of vicissitudes of imprinting. DNA may be identical in a donor and his/her reproductive clone, but the genes expressed would differ. That is, one's phenotype depends not upon the DNA *per se* but upon the genes expressed (i.e. the protein gene product). Thus, there can never be a true clone if epigenetic differences exist. In fact, this is already evident in cloned animals whose appearance is not identical to that of the donor.

To those who insist on distinct DNA, one could turn to a branch of cloning, somatic cell hybridization. Using this technology, infertile couples could have their genetically own biparental offspring.

The Need for Dialogue Before It's Too Late

Whether cloning is necessary will eventually be decided not strictly on *a priori* ethical grounds, but also on pragmatic medical ethics. In therapeutic cloning, the current dichotomy of opinion will probably continue until therapeutic success is demonstrated in regenerative medicine. Once this occurs, it will probably obviate the dichotomous stances of whether a blastocyst is a person or should simply be treated with respect. With success, qualms may dissipate. This outcome will thus recapitulate the experience observed with IVF and preimplantation genetic diagnosis. The public will embrace the new technology once it is shown to work.

In reproductive cloning, . . . the current proscription should continue on grounds of efficacy and safety, but it is important to appreciate that at present the public's attitude still represents reflex orthodoxy. Open discussion continues to be eschewed. This will probably continue until scientific advances demonstrate that reproductive cloning is safer and better than the alternatives (conventional assisted reproduction). If this proves to be true, one can argue that it would be unethical to withhold the technology. Given that this scenario is not implausible, the scientific community should embark upon a long delayed dialogue on reproductive cloning. In its absence, acceptance may occur 'on the ground' without real debate and without necessary restraints.

5

Therapeutic Cloning Is Moral

Katrien Devolder and Julian Savulescu

Katrien Devolder is a researcher with the Department of Philosophy and Moral Sciences at Ghent University in Belgium. She holds a doctorate degree in philosophy and focuses her studies on bioethics. Julian Savulescu is a philosopher and bioethicist who serves as a professor of ethics at the University of Oxford in England. He is known for his examinations of the ethical implications of cloning and embryonic stem cell research.

Therapeutic cloning involving stem cells is a significant part of modern medical research. Therapeutic cloning methods will aid organ and tissue transplantations by ensuring compatibility with replacements. Such research is also important because it can provide innumerable copies of cells upon which drug tests and disease therapies can be performed to address the needs of individual patients. Using cloned cells will even eliminate the need for clinical testing of drugs and other cures on research animals. Although there are moral arguments raised against cloning— especially involving stem cells, these objections are easily dismissed or otherwise fail to outweigh the ethical demand to act in order to save the lives of those burdened by diseases that could be cured by cloning and stem cell research.

The first reason [cloning and stem cell] research is important is that it is a leap toward self-transplantation. The objective of what is often indicated as "therapeutic cloning" is

Katrien Devolder and Julian Savulescu, "The Moral Imperative to Conduct Embryonic Stem Cell and Cloning Research," *Cambridge Quarterly of Healthcare Ethics*, vol. 15, January 2006, pp. 7–8, 10–19. Copyright © Cambridge University Press 2006. Reprinted with the permission of Cambridge University Press.

to produce pluripotent stem cells that carry the nuclear genome of the patient and then induce them to differentiate into replacement cells, such as cardiomyocytes to replace damaged heart tissue or insulin-producing beta-cells for patients with diabetes, or virtually any cell type, including sex cells. . . . Although cloning research is still in its infancy and much more research needs to be done, it may give us one day the possibility to produce "patient matched" tissue to repair damaged organs like the heart and brain, which have no capacity for regeneration, providing radical new treatments for stroke and heart attack, Parkinson's disease, and many other diseases. This is regenerative medicine. It is the Holy Grail of medicine.

Transplantation to Cure Disease

[Biotech scientist William] Rideout and colleagues recently reported the cure of a genetic disease using therapeutic cloning. They created a mouse with the Severe Combined Immunodeficiency (commonly known as the "boy in the bubble disease"). They took cells from the tail, subjected these to the cloning process, and produced ES [embryonic stem] cells in which the gene was introduced to correct the genetic defect. These were introduced back into the mouse, curing the disease. This is the proof of principle for the therapeutic benefits of cloning.

Cloning would facilitate [disease] research by making it possible to monitor the progress of the disease as it develops inside the cells.

Therapeutic cloning is important for several reasons:

1. There is a shortage of tissue for transplantation. As few as 5% of the organs needed ever become available, with the discrepancy between the number of potential recipients and donor organs increasing by approximately 10–15% each year in the United States.

2. There are problems with compatibility of transplanted tissue, requiring immunosuppressive therapy with serious side effects. Moreover, cloned tissue would be compatible without the infectious risks of xenotransplants.

3. The role of transplantation could be expanded to include common diseases like heart attack and stroke. After disease and injury, as occurs in stroke, the dead part of the brain is replaced by scar tissue, which serves only to maintain structural integrity. It does not function as brain would function. It may be possible in the future to use therapeutic cloning to give stroke victims new brain tissue, with full or partial functionality.

Providing Cellular Models to Study and Treat Disease

The second reason cloning research is important is because it opens up a whole new avenue of medical research. It could be used to study in a radically new way any disease in a culture dish. Cloning of a single skin cell could be used to produce inexhaustible amounts of cells and tissue from a patient with a certain disease. This tissue could be experimented upon to understand why disease occurs. It could be used to understand the genetic contribution to disease and to test vast arrays of new drugs. This would enable research that cannot be done in patients themselves or where there are too few patients to work with in the case of rare genetic diseases. At present, it is often impossible to safely take samples of affected cells from patients, especially those with genetic diseases that affect the brain or the heart. Ian Wilmut [the genetic scientist who first cloned a sheep] and his team want to create ES cell lines from embryos cloned from people with amyotropic lateral sclerosis (ALS), a currently incurable neurodegenerative condition. It is impossible to remove motor neurons from patients for study. Using cloning to create cultures of motor neurons from these patients would make it possible to investigate the cause of the disease and to test new therapies. Moreover, symptoms mostly develop after the disease has been progressing for some time, which makes the study of the cause of the disease more difficult. Cloning would facilitate this research by making it possible to monitor the progress of the disease as it develops inside the cells. It would also reduce the need for human and animal experimentation because human cells and tissues, not people or animals, could be used to test new drugs.

Cloning research could result in treatments for common diseases like heart disease, stroke, and cancer.

Other areas where this form of cloning would be very useful are the study of genetic variation and its interaction with environmental factors and the study of interactions between genes and drugs, the study of early human development and the underlying mechanisms regulating cell growth and differentiation, which would provide better knowledge and control over the manipulation and reprogramming of cells within patients, and the investigation of how pathogens interact with specific cell types, which would help us to understand how to use viruses as a vehicle for reintroducing healthy genes to a damaged body.

Most importantly, new treatments could be tested on the cells and tissues derived by cloning to test for safety and efficacy. Vast panels of potentially useful new chemotherapeutic agents could be tested, for example, on human cancer tissue without the need for extensive preliminary testing in animals or the dangerous exposure of humans to highly experimental drugs.

These two applications—self-transplantation and the development of cellular models of diseases—mean that cloning may be viewed as a scientific accomplishment on par with splitting the atom. But it will be vastly more beneficial to humanity. It may surpass the discovery of X-rays and penicillin.

A Moral Imperative to Act

James Rachels was one of the first writers to argue that we are morally responsible and blameworthy not merely for the foreseeable and avoidable consequences of our actions, but also for the foreseeable consequences of our omissions, or what we fail to do, when we could have reasonably acted otherwise. To fail to do beneficial research can be as wrong as doing harmful research.

Imagine that a scientific team, after 10 years of research, develops a cure for a disease that kills 100,000 people per year. Imagine that for one year, the team fights over who will have what fraction of the profits. As a consequence, the release of the drug is delayed by one year. Those scientists are as responsible for those deaths as if they had killed those 100,000 sick people. Now imagine that an ethics committee delays release of the drug because of concern over the consent process—the members are responsible for those patients' deaths if their concerns are not well grounded and significant. Imagine now that instead the delay is not at the completion but at the very beginning—politicians prevent the research from commencing for one year on some kind of moral grounds. Unless there are truly significant moral considerations, those politicians who cause the drug to be developed one year later than it could have been are responsible for those 100,000 deaths. To fail to develop a drug that will save 100,000 lives is morally equivalent to failing to release it. We may not be able to point to those people whose lives would have been saved, but their lives are no less valuable because they are in the future or they are anonymous. Cloning research could result in treatments for common diseases like heart disease, stroke, and cancer. It has a considerable potential to save hundreds of thousands if not millions of lives. Through a failure of moral imagination we may continue to hold back cloning research and be responsible for the deaths of many people who perished while we delayed the development of treatments. This research is of enormous potential benefit to humanity. This provides a strong prima facie [self-evident] case in favor not just of allowing cloning research, but positively supporting it through permissive legislation and generous public funding. The laws that prevent such lifesaving research may be, in a moral sense, lethal.

There are, however, serious ethical objections. We will consider five of the strongest objections, showing this new research casts many of these in a new light.

Objection 1: Protection of Human Life

The central objection to all ES cell and cloning research is that it represents the destruction of human life. At this time, it is not yet possible to extract ES cells without "killing" embryos.

The [United Nations] UN Declaration on Human Cloning calls upon Member States to "protect adequately human life" in the application of life sciences. The obvious question is what we understand "human life" and "adequate protection" to mean.

Some people believe that the human embryo is human life with the same moral value as a person. Therefore, embryos should never be used merely as a means, however beneficial the ends may be. "One may not heal by killing," said Cardinal Joachim Meisner with regard to ES cell research. Others think embryos have the potential to become a person, and therefore should be protected as if they were persons.

It is not our intention to review the enormous volume of debate on the issue of the moral status of the embryo. What we do want to point out here is that cloning research allows us to understand the objection with regard to destroying human life in a different light. Many countries permit research on so-called spare embryos, that is, embryos created during in vitro fertilization (IVF) that are no longer a part of a couple's reproductive plans. . . .

Embryos may have a special moral status when they are a part of a parental project. That is why it would be wrong to destroy the embryos of a couple trying to have a child with IVF. But when a couple's family is complete or they do not want children, the value people accord to embryos often decreases. That is why society allows and in some cases requires the destruction of embryos when infertile couples have completed their family using IVF, instead of requiring them to donate or adopt out those excess or spare embryos. And that is why the status of an embryo created for research is different from the status of an embryo created for the purposes of reproduction. Just as there are spare embryos not required for reproduction, so too there are "spare eggs" that are surplus to reproductive needs. . . .

Reproductive cloning is unlikely to ever be safe.

Women are born with millions of eggs and hundreds of thousands of eggs perish during their reproductive life as they will only have a limited number of, usually 1–3, children. Women have a right to control their reproduction and are not obliged to have as many children as they could possibly have. These eggs would never have produced a baby. Instead of perishing for no reason, they were used to produce highly valuable stem cells.

We have argued that there is a difference between the moral status of embryos created intentionally as a part of project to have a child ("wanted embryos") and those created unintentionally or for the purposes of research ("unwanted embryos"). Yet many people will continue to view embryos as children, and so not accept this distinction. But there is another way in which cloning research could be done without using human embryos at all. We could remove the nucleus from a rabbit egg. DNA of a human skin cell could be introduced in a nuclear transfer procedure (cloning). This chimera of a rabbit egg and human DNA would never develop into a living being—it stops development early in embryonic development at the stage when tissues are formed. However, human embryonic stem cells can be extracted from this construct and experimented upon to form cellular models of human disease. Since the entity produced would never continue development, no embryo would have been formed. This cloning research would not destroy a human embryo.

Objection 2: Cloning Is Unnecessary

Republican Senator Brownback, who introduced the Human Cloning Prohibition Act of 2003 in the United States, stated that "human cloning is immoral and completely unnecessary. Recent advances in adult and non-embryonic stem cell research are showing that real results are being achieved without reliance on controversial human cloning technology."

This claim is false. Adult stem cells could not be used to produce cellular models of human disease as cloning and the production of embryonic stem cell lines could. This is a critical new line of research.

Therapeutic cloning may cure [chronic] diseases and not just treat them.

Adult stem cells have been found in several tissues of the human body, including skin, bone marrow, blood, the brain, and many others. [Bioengineer Geza] Kogler and colleagues identified human adult stem cells from the umbilical cord blood with intrinsic pluripotent differentiation potential. There is a growing consensus among scientists on the great value of cord blood stem cells for transplantation. Over the past years there have been extensive discussions on which line of research is *most* promising. Those opposing ES cell research have often stated that ES cell research is not necessary because the same research goals can be reached with adult stem cells. However, work [since 2004] has convincingly demonstrated that adult stem cells will not replace ES cells. Both cell types are different; they both have their advantages and disadvantages and will be useful for particular purposes. In some cases, combined ES cell and adult stem cell therapy might be the best option. Therefore, further research is required on both cell types. . . .

Objection 3: Slippery Slope to Reproductive Cloning

Another objection to cloning research is that this brings us "one step closer" to human reproductive cloning—cloning to produce babies. In his statement "Farming humans for fun" Richard Doerflinger, of the U.S. Conference of Catholic Bishops, said that "human cloning's slippery slope toward complete dehumanization of human beings will not stop until the U.S. Senate passes Senator Brownback's complete ban on human cloning." Leon Kass, President of the President's Council on Bioethics, called for federal legislation to stop human cloning for any purpose. He stated that "the age of human cloning has apparently arrived: today, cloned blastocysts for research, tomorrow cloned blastocysts for babymaking."

Reproductive cloning is unlikely to ever be safe. This is based on observation of cloned animals (mostly mice and cows) that have hundreds of genes that are abnormally expressed, in particular genes important for fetal development (so called imprinted genes). This results in abnormalities during development (95% or more of cloned embryos abort), at birth ("large offspring syndrome"), or later in life (even seemingly normal mice often develop obesity, die prematurely, or develop tumors compared with controls). It has been said that there are "biological barriers" to reproductive cloning. Interestingly, cloning to produce stem cells should be safe because the genes that cause the cloned embryos to be abnormal are not important for the derivation of ES cells (there is no fetal development). In addition, the isolation of ES cells is a selection process where "normal" cells will grow out into an ES cell line whereas "abnormal" (not fully reprogrammed cells) will be selected against.

The response to fears about reproductive cloning is not to ban cloning altogether. It is to ban reproductive cloning. . . .

The slippery slope argument is, in many cases a specious one, which is intended to conceal the lack of serious reasoning. The image of a slippery slope is misleading. If a metaphor must be used then we should speak of a staircase on which we could descend, step by step, until we have reached a certain level. Some levels are desirable, others are not. There is no reason why we should not be able to remain on a certain level and consider calmly whether or not we want to take the next step. . . .

Objection 4: Economic and Social Justice Considerations

Stem cell and cloning research have huge economic potential—California has injected US$3 billion into this research. However, there remain important economic and social justice objections to this research. The research is sometimes said to be a Western luxury, which will be unaffordable to most of the world. It is unjust to devote limited resources to such research.

Indeed, the UN appears seduced by this worry. Its Declaration on Human Cloning, in its final point, calls upon Member States, "in their financing of medical research, including life sciences, to take into account the pressing global issues such as HIV/AIDS, tuberculosis and malaria, which affect in particular the developing countries."

The objection regarding justice is more acute in light of the following three alleged problems with cloning research.

Unsafe. There are numerous unanswered questions as to the control of ES cell growth and differentiation. ES cells have the potential to be tumorigenic, growing into teratomas and teratocarcinomas when injected into mice. Research is being done on this worldwide and progress is being made.

Recent research shows there may be infectious and other risks, such as occurred with BSE [bovine spongiform encephalopathy, or mad cow disease], of transplanting such tissue back to people, when it is grown on foreign culture material.

Labor intensive and expensive. Anne McLaren, the famous British geneticist, remarked that therapeutic cloning would probably be a realistic option only for the very rich and that "any such personalized treatment will always remain labor intensive, and hence, expensive." "Clone-ialism" is the pejorative term that extends this idea: Medically advanced countries will try to exploit less advanced ones and biotechnology will facilitate this trend.

But current treatments and care for patients suffering from chronic diseases for which ES cell therapies may be used are also expensive and labor intensive. Moreover, therapeutic cloning may cure these diseases and not just treat them. Therapies are also likely to become cheaper, easier, and accessible to more people after some time.

The whole cloning procedure takes a long time and some clinical applications may not allow for this (e.g., myocardial infarction, acute liver failure, or traumatic or infectious spinal cord damage). Therapeutic cloning would likely be reserved for chronic conditions.

Apart from this, as Ian Wilmut has pointed out, "[N]ot all diseases are equal in terms of expense, and treatments could be targeted to maximize benefit. An older person with heart disease, for example, could be treated with stem cells that are not a genetic match, take drugs to suppress their immune system for the rest of their life, and live with the side-effects. A younger person might benefit from stem cells that match exactly."

The exploitation of women. If cloning with embryos were permitted, it would require, to be effective, a large number of eggs or oocytes. In a speech of the Holy See to the UN, Archbishop Migliore stated that, "[T]he process of obtaining these eggs, which is not without risk, would use women's bodies as mere reservoirs of oocytes, instrumentalizing women and undermining their dignity."

The UN Declaration on Human Cloning also stresses this point and calls upon Member States to take measures to prevent the exploitation of women in the application of life sciences.

However, the problem of the need for large numbers of eggs from women is likely to be a short-term problem for several reasons. First, one of the main purposes of cloning is to perform research to understand how cells develop and can be reprogrammed to an immature state. Once that is understood, the process can be replicated in a laboratory and there will be no need for new eggs. Second, researchers are investigating the use of alternatives, including fetal oocytes and eggs from adult ovaries, obtained postmortem or during an operation. In June 2005, a team of Belgian scientists reported at the annual conference of the European Society of Human Reproduction and Embryology (ESHRE) that they had cloned human embryos using human eggs matured in the laboratory. They hope one day this will make it possible to perform therapeutic cloning by creating artificial eggs from patients' body cells. Another alternative is the differentiation of ES cells in culture into germ cells and full-grown oocytes. Scientists from the University of Sheffield stated at the ESHRE conference that human ES cells can develop into primordial germ cells—the cells that eventually become eggs or sperm. Recent studies have found that mammals may continue to produce new eggs throughout their lives. If "ovary stem cells" really exist, this could make it possible to produce more eggs. Another option researchers are investigating is the use of nonhuman oocytes, such as frog eggs, for the purpose of cloning research. Another possibility is to ask people undergoing IVF to donate one or two of their eggs. These women undergo the risk of hormone stimulation anyhow. The research team at the University of Newcastle upon Tyne has received permission to ask IVF patients to give up two eggs from each batch collected for their treatment.

Of course, if self-transplantation is perfected, families, eager to help their dying or sick relative, may well volunteer sufficient eggs for the treatment of their sick relative.

There Is No Evidence of Injustice

These three considerations have led some to suggest that it is unjust and wrong to do cloning research. As we have suggested, each of these specific objections may have solutions in the future. But, most importantly, *none of these considerations applies to the second application of cloning research: to provide cellular models for human disease.* This will enable research into and the development of drugs to treat common diseases, like cancer and heart disease, which afflict people all over the world. These drugs may be inexpensive. Concerns about infection and safety do not apply to this research as it is about understanding disease and developing drugs in a laboratory where there would be no chance of infection. It is not labor intensive—it is experimenting on cells and tissues, which is done now in animals. It would not require large numbers of eggs as a few eggs would produce inexhaustible amounts of tissue to study a particular disease, since embryonic stem cells produce immortal cell lines. Insofar as these objections have force, they only have force against cloning for self-transplantation, not cloning for developing cellular models of human disease.

Objection 5: Disruption of the Moral Fabric of Society

There are concerns that this research is moving too fast and the community is not ready to accept it. People in society hold different values and these differing values must be respected. Concerns that moral fabric and cohesiveness of society will be torn apart provide reasons for care and reflection. But precaution must be balanced against delay in developing life-saving treatments. We must remember that the lives of many innocent children and adults are at stake. We believe that an understanding of the differences between reproductive cloning and cloning for the purposes of research and therapy, if properly understood, would allay the concerns of many citizens. Moreover, understanding the concept of cloning to produce models of human disease, to test new treatments, should convince some of the legitimate scientific merits of this research. Further strategies to promote community acceptance and cohesiveness include:

1. Transparency. High quality, clear information about the research and its limitations. The public must understand the science.

2. Public control and predictability. People fear that scientists are opening Pandora's box. There must be some predictability and sense of control over the research.

3. Legislative control. Related to [objection] 2, bans on reproductive cloning are required to achieve control over the application of this research.

4. Independent oversight. Apart from legislation, the public may require independent oversight of scientists, through ethics committees of licensing bodies such as the HFEA [Human Fertilisation and Embryology Authority] and the Embryonic Stem Cell Research Oversight (ESCRO) committee proposed by the National Academy of Sciences in their report "Guidelines for Human Embryonic Stem Cell Research."

5. Review. The field is rapidly evolving and there is a need to frequently review the adequacy of controls.

6. Participation and respect for value diversity. Individuals and cultures have different values. It is important that those different values be respected through giving individuals and particular cultures a voice and formulating the research in light of those concerns.

7. Reassurance and demonstration of benefit. People need reassurance that the risks are being managed and that benefits are occurring. Most importantly, the public needs to see that these benefits are returning to citizens.

The Race Has to Be Run

There are good reasons to pursue cloning research. There is potential to increase immeasurably scientific understanding of cellular development and control. There is the potential to revolutionize the practice of transplantation medicine, which may significantly prolong human life. Understanding the two different applications of cloning—self-transplantation and the development of cellular models of disease—helps us to address many of the objections. Cloning to produce cellular models of disease would require relatively few eggs to produce vast amounts of tissue for the study of disease. This may result in the development of drugs for common conditions that afflict people all around the world, including in the developing world. And finally, there would be no risk of infection from drugs developed by studying tissue in this way as the drug molecules would be produced pharmaceutically. Cloning research can be pursued using spare eggs that would not interfere with reproduction. Using animal eggs, oocytes grown in the laboratory, or stem cell derived eggs would avoid the problem of egg shortage entirely.

The critical point is that we cannot predict in advance the results of scientific research. What this research turns up may be very different from what is promised. But it may be very important nonetheless. There is an important distinction between the regulation of research and the formation of social policy and law. Research should only be prevented if it harms people or exposes them to unreasonable risks. This research does not harm any person. It only stands to benefit people. We must do the research, then form the policy on the basis of the results, not in advance of them, not in prediction of them, and not in fear of them. Scientific research is like trying to pick the winner of a horse race. There can be favorites, but one can never know in advance which horse will win. The race has to be run.

6

Therapeutic Cloning
Is Immoral

Kate Cregan

Kate Cregan is a research fellow at the School of Culture and Communication at the University of Melbourne in Australia. She studies early modern anatomy and embodiment across history. She is the author of The Theatre of the Body: Staging Death and Embodying Life in Early Modern London.

Although religious objections to therapeutic cloning may be valid, a larger sense of human morality rejects this type of cloning because it alters notions of conception and mortality. It reduces embryos into materials for transplants or genetic therapies. In addition, the rationale for such treatments implies that people with potentially curable disabilities are living less worthwhile lives, and it turns the cloning community into the arbiter of what is normal and acceptable in society. To accept such changes would require the world—or at least those parts that could afford to have access to these therapies—to redefine what it is to be human and to conclude that the wonder of life has much to do with how well it can be manipulated by science.

Debates, around embryonic stem cells, polarize around religious concerns and bioethical rejections of those concerns, by and large. However, this is a false dichotomy fostered by a media driven by a desire for easy answers and news grabs. It is possible to find embryonic stem cell technology problematic without resorting to religious objections or narrow arguments from the 'sanctity of life'.

Kate Cregan, "Ethical and Social Issues of Embryonic Stem Cell Technology," *Internal Medicine Journal*, vol. 35, pp. 126–127, 2005. Copyright © 2005 Basil Blackwell Ltd. Reproduced by permission of Blackwell Publishers Ltd.

Of greater concern is the place that embryos and embryonic stem cell technology holds within a larger social complex. It does not require religious belief or affiliation to recognize that we belong to a wider society that has embedded and embodied traditions about how we come together as social beings and how we produce and reproduce society. How we treat the bases of human life, particularly if we are drawn into technologizing and/or commercializing them, has wider implications. My concern is that we risk turning those embedded social traditions into instrumental matter open to economic speculation, and at what cost?

On an immediate, pragmatic level ... therapeutic cloning could lead to the rank commercialization and exploitation of women.

Altering What It Means to Be Human

Embryonic stem cell technology and therapeutic cloning have the potential to alter, fundamentally, the social meaning of both human conception and human mortality. In some of its projected outcomes, such as turning embryos into transferable post-human body matter, or developing 'therapeutic cloning' as a way of industrializing the availability of transplantable body parts, it bypasses hitherto foundational assumptions by which we live and die as embodied persons. In all of this, the aim of the new technology is to satisfy individualistic desires for transcending faulty body parts and to make market gains out of remaking life-chances. In this sense, the current debate over the limits of technological intervention is no less than a defining moment in the history of how we are to understand the meaning of living as human beings. It contributes to reducing basic ontological questions to the search for a new philosopher's stone.

The most common arguments for embryonic stem cell technology, and in particular therapeutic cloning, are that, first, it gives hope of treatment or cure for many diseases; second that the embryos that researchers would be working on are at a very early stage of development and finally that ethics bodies already allow research on embryos up to 14 days for the improvement of *in vitro* fertilization. These points are put forward as sufficient reasons to allow researchers to pursue their research.

The general tenor of the case in favour of embryonic stem cell research has been to argue that the embryos subjected to research processes are not sentient or rights-bearing individuals. Early embryos are of little moral significance, therefore (double negatively), there is *not* sufficient reason *not* to proceed with treating embryos as a research resource. On balance, the pro-therapeutic-cloning ethicists have presented a utilitarian case that if the products of human embryonic stem cell research *might* potentially treat diseases such as Parkinson's disease, Alzheimer's disease and diabetes, or in related arguments that pre-implantation diagnostic screening will prevent the birth of disabled children, the decision weighs more heavily in favour of proceeding than not. This is not a strong ethical argument in itself. However, in the context of the strategies being used to naturalize the techno-scientific possibilities, for instance by naming individuals such as Christopher Reeve and your grand-mother as persons who might benefit, it carries considerable force in the media-saturated community.

Exploiting Poor Women

The outcomes are supposedly, pancreatic cells for diabetes, nerve cells for Parkinson's disease, heart cells for cardiac disease. It is far from clear that the promises are ever likely to be fulfilled. As has been reiterated by scientists and ethicists alike, the problems inherent, even in medical theory, are serious (the possibility of the implanted cells spontaneously mutating and forming tumours being just one issue), and the ethics are fraught. For example, as Professor Alan Trounson, one of the leading Australian stem cell researchers, has said, treating any of these diseases with tailored therapeutically cloned cells would require massive harvesting of human eggs. While Professor Trounson has proposed the fusion of an individual's cells with already derived embryonic stem cells as a way of getting around this need for eggs (and any number of other *theoretical* possibilities), there are still many researchers who do want to therapeutically clone—not least because it is practicably possible. National governments worldwide and even the UN [United Nation] General Assembly have either enacted legislation to regulate therapeutic cloning or propose to do so. So the questions remain: who would be most likely to 'donate' their eggs, and why? The answer is obvious: poor women, quite possibly from countries with less stringent (or no) legal prohibition against such exploitation, would be the most likely candidates. On an immediate, pragmatic level then, therapeutic cloning could lead to the rank commercialization and exploitation of women, most probably poor or developing world women, to provide the raw materials for the treatment of developed world diseases. It could lead to a global trade in human eggs. Indeed, these and other techno-medical research processes are already subject to international interests and globalizing influences.

An Exclusive Technology

Nor is it clear whose lives would be made better by these therapies, in practice. We know very well, with the pressure to recoup research and development funding, that those in the poorer sections of the developed world and the vast majority of those in the developing world are unlikely to have access to any of this technology, if it ever finds a viable application. We have learned this much at least from a long history of pharmaceutical conglomerates withholding generic therapies in the quest for profit, the wrangling over AIDS medications in South Africa being just one example, and dumping unsafe drugs on developing world markets.

The highly emotive and, in some cases, frankly exploitative use of individual sufferers of diseases in an attempt to sway a confused public and parliament, obliterates the social background, the social processes and the social consequences of these proposed technologies. Is it worth fundamentally altering the way we see ourselves and the way we see each other, either on the overblown hope of satisfying individual desires to live longer or to make global pharmaceutical conglomerates a profit out of individually tailored drug-testing 'body matter'? Embryonic stem cell technology re-presents our bodies as fetishized objects that only scientists know how to treat effectively. If we uncritically accept embryonic stem-cell technology, we invite the rationalization of our embodiment. More generally, we participate in removing our bodies/ourselves from the context and the labour of our reproduction, the human setting that brings us into being in the first place. More fundamentally, just because someone has a debilitating disease, it does not mean that his or her life is not worth living.

The Wonder of Life Is Not Its Ease of Manipulation

The fears and desires of individuals to live longer or healthier are not unreasonable in themselves. However, they too mask the terms of the production of what are ephemeral possibilities of treatments; they depend on society as a whole redefining our historically lived understanding of what it is to be or become a human being. Like organs removed from the reality of the death of the person from whom they came, embryonic stem cell technology removes reproduction from the reality of the people who have created a life. Ova, sperm, embryos are removed—abstracted—from the conditions of their production; persons in relationship, no matter what that relationship may consist in. The bodily emissions of two people came together to create a life-form that, if left to its own devices in the appropriate environment, has a good chance of becoming a new human being. The techno-scientific re-creation of human embryonic stem cells overrides this basic condition even if it proclaims to be mere therapy.

Accepting the products of techno-science, including the potential of organs grown in stem-cell laboratories, is not simply a matter of personal choice. It is intimately connected with how we perceive each other, our ability to reproduce ourselves and our societies. These products provide another means of re-presenting us to ourselves, distancing us from face-to-face, embodied relations. The tensions at work in this are apparent, even in the arguments that come from the mouths of scientific researchers. We are told that the human matter at stake to be experimented upon is a tenth of the size of the head of a pin and is therefore morally inconsequential. At the same time, we are shown in living colour the miraculousness of the first days after conception being probed and stem cells removed. Even the researchers cannot make up their minds. They want us to accept that 'surplus embryos' are worthless blobs of cells destined for the sink—waste cells that should be put to good use, and at the same time they ask us to reward their efforts in manipulating them, because they are dealing with miraculous bundles of cells that can do the most amazing things in differentiating into all the cells that make up the complete human body. Are they wondrous because they are human, or is the meaning of being human in yet another area of techno-science being reduced to its wondrous manipulability?

7

Reproductive Cloning Would Strengthen the American Family

Gregory E. Pence

A professor of philosophy at the University of Alabama at Birmingham, Gregory E. Pence is the author of The Elements of Bioethics, Cloning After Dolly, Brave New Bioethics, *and other books. In his work, Pence explores the ethical issues associated with technological advances in medical fields.*

Those who oppose cloning contend that regardless of how safe the technology and procedure may become in the future, cloning itself can never be justified for moral, ethical, and spiritual reasons. However, many of these critics fail to recognize the benefits that reproductive cloning would produce in terms of strengthening the family unit and society in general. Cloned children would be among the most wanted and happiest in the world, which in turn would serve to strengthen the family structure that brought them into being. Further, these stronger families and happier individuals would create a happier society.

A [2003] news release described how a group of professionals approached the World Court, urging it to make reproductive cloning a crime against humanity. Such a move assumes that, regardless of how safe it becomes, reproductive

Gregory E. Pence, *Cloning After Dolly: Who's Still Afraid?* Lanham, MD: Rowman & Littlefield, 2004. Copyright © 2004 by Rowman & Littlefield Publishers, Inc. All rights reserved. Reproduced by permission.

cloning is not wrong because of its lack of safety at present or because the early stage of science now produces too many abnormalities, but because reproductive cloning is intrinsically wrong in itself.

This is not a scientific claim but a philosophical one. Although made by scientists, it lands in that more general realm known as ordinary morality, as do claims about the conduct of physicians who may want to be judged only by the norms internal to medicine but are still judged by norms of truth telling, decency, respect for persons, and fairness that stem from ordinary morality.

Wrong, Regardless of Safety

Several common arguments assert that reproductive cloning is intrinsically wrong, each with a slightly different twist and in different words but all amounting to the same claim—regardless of how safe it becomes or how much good it might create for a particular family, reproductive cloning is essentially wrong. These arguments include the following: reproductive cloning is an evil practice in itself; it inherently destroys the dignity of the child created; it is incompatible with the sanctity of life; it is against the will of God; it inherently dehumanizes children and treats them as commodities; it is evil because one kind of being is used as a resource for another.

A different class of arguments does not claim that reproductive cloning is intrinsically wrong but asserts that it is nevertheless wrong because it *indirectly* leads to bad consequences to the child, the couple, or society. Here reproductive cloning is claimed to be wrong because it is psychologically bad in some way for the cloned child or because the genes of the cloned child may have some hidden abnormality that may not be expressed until adulthood.

Or it is claimed that cloning is harmful to the parents who create a child with strong expectations, or it is wrong to start a practice in society where children are not loved in themselves as God's gifts but treated as commodities designed to bioengineering specifications.

Finally, critics argue that reproductive cloning is indirectly wrong because of its indirect, long-term consequences for society: that it leads to decreased genetic diversity in the human gene pool, that it sends the wrong message to the disabled, and that it will eventually send the wrong message to normals that there is something wrong about them. . . .

Now I want to turn to the more difficult task of making the strongest possible argument, once animal studies make it safe to try, *for* reproductive cloning.

For the sake of conceptual clarity, in the following pages I assume that one day has come when all mammals and especially primates can be routinely and safely originated by cloning with a rate of defects no higher than that found in sexual reproduction in the same species. I assume that studies of cloned human embryos have shown that they can be created in the same way, without any more abnormalities than occur in sexual reproduction. All that assumed, what's the case for allowing safe, human reproductive cloning?

Considering the Importance of Planning Conception

The first argument needs a little background, so let's detour a moment and consider the oft heard claim that an adolescent or adult will be traumatized to learn that he or she was adopted, was created by in vitro fertilization, has an unknown twin, was created by insemination of donor sperm, or was originated by cloning. As I have already argued, these claims are highly speculative and mostly express the projections of critics.

These critics have us imaging a future when cloned children spend hours brooding over the fact that their parents willed their existence and consciously thought about whose genotype they would embody. They envision such children agonizing over whether they will live up to their parents' expectations, traumatized by the fear that they will not and trembling lest they lose their parents' love.

How silly! To see why, we need not go far into the future but merely turn the mirror on ourselves, for there is one question close at hand that is foundational to anyone who was born before 1965: were we really wanted by our parents or were we just accidents? Were we consciously wanted, planned, and deliriously sought after, or were we an unintended-but-foreseeable by-product of having unprotected sex in an age when both contraception and abortion were illegal for all couples, married or not?

First, even if we ask our parents and they swear we were wanted (what would you say to *your* kids?), we will really never know. Second, we don't really care about the answer and probably won't ask our parents, but either way, given all the water under the bridge, the answer is irrelevant.

Nor do we ask our parents whether they really wanted a girl instead of a boy. We don't ask them if they planned to have a child but only years later, once they had their marriage on a better footing or had more money. We don't ask if they thought about adopting instead of conceiving, and if when young they considered a childless lifestyle that involved traveling around the world to exotic locations.

To the extent that children created by cloning are happy, the general happiness in the world increases.

No, we usually don't ask such questions and if we do, our parents are usually a bit uncomfortable (Why are you asking me *that?*). Bonding, affection, and the life of the family have long since carried us beyond such questions, smoothing over unexpected answers. Most of us happily come to believe that our creation was in the stars, just as it should have been.

The Most Wanted Children in Human History

One day children created by cloning will be as indifferent to their origins as we post-1965-born adults are today. So too for their families, bonding, affection, and the life of the family will have long since carried them beyond such questions, smoothing over unexpected problems.

Compare adults created by in vitro fertilization, for whom we now have a twenty-five-year history. As we know, their special origins to them are no big deal: they are just glad to be alive; indeed, many know they are among the most loved children in human history.

Likewise, and to a much greater degree, originating children by safe cloning will spare them any traumas associated with uncertainty about being wanted. With the exception of firstborn sons of childless monarchs of great kingdoms, such children may be the most wanted, most anticipated children in history.

Safe cloning will be intrinsically good for children in giving them a deep, rich sense that their parents sincerely wanted them.

Children created by in vitro fertilization also know they were wanted, but children created by safe cloning have additional assurance because they were wanted not just as generic children but for their general characteristics. Not only will Faith know that Mom and Dad wanted her to exist, but will know that they wanted a girl with a genetic predisposition to strong religious belief. ("Mom and Daddy always wanted a faith-based girl, so the Lord gave them a way to make me. I love them so much and I sure know they love me.")

Safe cloning will be intrinsically good for children in giving them a deep, rich sense that their parents sincerely wanted them, not only as their firstborn child but also as a their first-born child with musical talent. Wrapped in parental reassurance, such children might be more self-confident and self-assured than normal children, who must (if they think about it) be uncertain about why they were created.

Beneath everyone's fears about designer babies and unrealistic parental expectations lies something that is different and good: the idea that children are wanted with a white-hot intensity. That is a very new, unusual idea to most people (except perhaps those who are familiar with clinics for assisted reproduction). We need time to be comfortable with the idea that children need not "just come" but can be intensely wanted. Even when parents don't get everything they want, we will learn that wanting kids intensely is a good thing.

Happier People and a Happier Society

A second argument that reproductive cloning could be in the intrinsic good of children needs a little rope, but not too much. That rope is the assumption that human genetics, proteinomics, and knowledge of functional gene-environment interactions will increasingly reveal not only the causes of bad states, such as depression and hypercholesterolemia, but also of good states, such as being good-natured, generally healthy, and long-lived.

Give me that same assumption here and see if I hang myself. But it's not fair to argue with the assumption that we will come to know which set of genes predisposes people to be happy, healthy, and long-lived. So let's say we do know these genes and how to safely choose them in a child originated by cloning.

Then, ceteris paribus, it would be intrinsically good for the child to have genes that predispose her to being happy, healthy, and long-lived rather than genes that predispose her to being morose and sick, and to die early. Such genes indeed may be *foundational* for a happy life, something that over time we come to see as each child's birthright. One day in the future, getting a healthy gene pack will be like getting fluoride in the water to prevent cavities or getting standard vaccinations against deadly childhood diseases.

Moreover, to the extent that children created by cloning are happy, the general happiness in the world increases. To the extent that their happiness makes their parents, friends, siblings, grandparents, spouses, and their own children happy, their happiness spreads in expanding circles, creating more happiness. All of this is intrinsically good.

Creating Stronger Families

A third kind of argument why reproductive cloning could be an intrinsic good builds on the assumption that creating wanted families is intrinsically good. Make this pro-life, pro-family assumption; if we do so, then safe reproductive cloning will almost certainly be a new kind of tool to use to create such families.

The strongest affirmation of the intrinsic good of reproductive cloning would be if children created by cloning used the same method . . . to create their own children.

Just as insemination of husband's sperm (AIH), anonymous sperm donation (AID), in vitro fertilization (IVF), surrogacy, and ooycte donation were all initially condemned and have now come to be accepted as useful tools in family making, so reproductive cloning one day will be seen the same way. For the one in eleven American couples who are infertile after two years of trying to conceive, how a baby gets created matters very little compared to the fact that the baby has been created.

Another reason why reproductive cloning may come to be seen as intrinsically good and why it should never be taken off the table and treated as a federal crime is that, as environmental toxins and delayed age of attempting first conception rises, citizens of developed societies may one day soon need better tools to aid them in creating children. Canadian sociologists Louise Vandelac and Marie-Helen Bacon of the University of Quebec-Montreal argue that soaring use of environmental pollutants around the world has dramatically decreased fertility in advanced societies. According to these sociologists, increasing breast cancer and endometriosis, as well as declining animal and human sperm counts and potencies, have been "directly associated with the sharp increase in pesticide use and environmental organochlorine chemicals such as polychlorinated biphenyls (PCBs) and hexachlorobenzene (HCB)."

Don't ban reproductive cloning! If we keep polluting our world, as we seem unable to stop doing, we may all be infertile one day and need an asexual way to reproduce humans. (This gives rise to another linkage argument on the other side: clean up the environment or you'll have to accept cloning!)

Cloning as a tool might prevent divorce. Some marriages fall apart owing to a lack of children. In some cases children bind two adults together, getting them over rough times for the sake of the children. This is true for adopted children also; so it is not necessary that the couple created the children themselves.

For some Orthodox Jews and Muslims, being unable to have children is a real curse, in part because the culture and the traditions, to a great extent, revolve around having a family. In such a culture, finding meaning without a family may be difficult. Less commonly, a particular kind of family is highly desired. For example, some marriages may dissolve because only girls are created and no boys. Although feminists argue that cloning should not support sexist choices, isn't it better to have a family based on consenting sexist choices than a divorced single mom or dad? Besides, personal life needs to be cut some space from pervasive moral criticism.

Insurance for Families

Another argument may be called the insurance argument. *Washington Post* columnist Abigail Trafford writes that 70,000 American kids under age twenty-five die every year, leaving their families devastated. Previous generations of Americans had large families and frequently experienced the death of a child. Now the birthrate has fallen to 2.13 children for every woman, and many women only bear one child. If that child dies, a woman may be past her reproductive age. For example, Katherine Gordon of Great Falls, Montana, whose seventeen-year-old daughter Emily was killed in a car accident in 1997, wants to clone Emily's genes to create a child. "I know it wouldn't be Emily—it would be her twin sister," she says.

Yes, Trafford agrees, many people find reproductive cloning repugnant, but many medical procedures are more repugnant. We tolerate them to save our lives or, in some cases, to try to create life. In her own case, her maternal grandmother died at age twenty giving birth to her mother, who was raised by her maternal grandparents in Ohio as a late child. Her aunts and uncle treated her as a baby sister and she blended into the family. So life is full of both disasters and surprises, and if we really value families and children, why should we not keep, as insurance, one tool for re-creating both?

Cloned Having Cloned Children

For the next argument for the intrinsic goodness of safe cloning, we should imagine not the forward-looking consent of cloned children (since it's nonsensical to talk of the consent of a being who does not exist about whether he should exist) but the backward-looking endorsement of cloned children. Call this the argument from *presumed consent.*

If cloned children later are told of their unique origins, told about why they were created and why their parents chose a particular genotype, and if such children endorse their method of origination, that would certainly be an argument in favor of this method. If most children created by cloning approve of their unique origins, then we can presume their consent for their origination.

The strongest affirmation of the intrinsic good of reproductive cloning would be if children created by cloning used the same method as adults to create their own children. They would not necessarily or even probably clone their own genotypes, but they might indeed clone someone's. If so, we would have something like rich, deep presumed consent. . . .

The Benefits of Change

Cloning would expand the currently small range of choices about creating children. It would also demystify the process of making children, taking the religious mumbo jumbo out of creation. Consider an analogy: imagine if the only way you could get a car (and this may have been true at one time in some communist countries) was through a lottery from the central allocation authority. If you were a fatalist, you would accept whatever you got, saying, "It's God's will that I drive a Hyundai."

Present conception is a lot like that. Whether you get a child, and what characteristics it has, are determined by other factors, not the parents. Many people now see that as a good thing and think it bad that parents might soon be able to control the kind of kids they have. But that is because everything is new and people fear that parents wouldn't love children chosen for their traits. But just as people once feared that parents wouldn't love their children if the children were planned, so too people will learn that chosen children will be loved more, not less, than those who came unplanned and unchosen.

Because cloning involves a choice about which genotype to reproduce, it would remove the arbitrariness of genetic roulette in sexual reproduction. It would put our growing knowledge of biology and genetics, not religion, behind choices about children. Although religion may be a force for good once children exist, it has generally been a force for evil in blocking scientific ways to overcome infertility or new ways of creating them. Reproductive fatalism is a flawed worldview, asserting that people should accept disease, dysfunction, and infertility. But this is false; all the above are human evils and medicine's enemies.

Reproductive fatalism holds that the status quo is natural and good. Although life now is much better than it was two or three hundred years ago, we know that life now is as good as it gets. To change any more, especially by adopting radical new kinds of biotechnology, is to risk losing everything.

That view is silly. It is almost certainly true that the present state of humanity can be improved in a thousand important ways. No one deserves to be sick, crippled, or barren. No one desires to die from old age or disease. Reproductive fatalists say we don't know enough, are not wise enough, to know when to change. But change in itself is not bad; we should adopt an experimental attitude toward change: judge each change by its consequences. Changes can be reversed if they work out badly (Prohibition, untaxed cigarettes).

Humans Will Be Responsible with Cloning

Nor are the most primitive ways of conceiving children the best ("It was good enough for me"). Having lots of ways to create wanted children is good. Some people will always use the most primitive ways; others will study all available options and choose the methods best for them. For still others, need will drive their choice.

Humans are not, as reproductive fatalists subtly imply, basically bad. When most of us think about it, we really don't believe anymore in Augustine's view of original sin, that human nature is tainted by terrible flaws deep within. No, humans are basically neutral to good. Yes, they are self-interested and possess only limited altruism, but that just proves that humans are neither saints nor perfect. Humans do have the moral ability to judge each case affecting them from experience, compassion, and reasoning, and then to blend many values to get the best answer. This is also true about choices about reproduction.

Similarly, reproductive fatalists and liberals do not want to trust parents to make choices about children, especially traits of children. They see all parents as potential child abusers who need to be monitored by the state. But that view is false to most experience. Most parents are good and want the best for their kids. Hence we can trust most parents without state interference or state regulation to make the best decisions about when and how to create children and how to raise them. . . .

Once the emotion and sensationalism are stripped from the topic of safe, reproductive human cloning, it is surprisingly easy to justify as something intrinsically good for humans. That is because it would be just another tool in our reproductive tool kit for creating families and better humans. And how can those two things not be good?

8

Reproductive Cloning Would Weaken the American Family

Stanley Kurtz

Stanley Kurtz, a fellow at both the Hudson Institute and the Hoover Institution, researches and writes on the "culture war" in America, focusing on issues relating to the family, feminism, homosexuality, affirmative action, and campus "political correctness." His articles have been published in the National Review Online, Policy Review, *the* Wall Street Journal, *and* Commentary.

While individuals oppose reproductive cloning for numerous ethical and religious reasons, one critique has largely been left out of government and public discussion of the issue: the probability that cloning will create more single-parent families. Because reproductive cloning does not require a man and a woman to conceive a child, many individuals in the United States will undoubtedly pursue cloning as a method of procreation out of wedlock. As a result, more children will be raised by single parents, which negatively impacts not only those children, but also society at large, because most observers agree that the best method for raising children is within a two-parent family structure. Reproductive cloning should be opposed because it has a significant potential to undermine the traditional American family.

Something is missing from *Human Cloning and Human Dignity*, the report of the President's Council on Bioethics: recognition of the harm reproductive cloning would do to the structure of the American family.

The omission is remarkable because this is surely one of the strongest arguments against cloning. *Human Cloning and Human Dignity* has been widely lauded for its fair and thorough coverage of the arguments on both sides of the cloning issue. The report even says that, when it comes to presenting these arguments, the council has decided to err on the side of inclusion. Nonetheless, the report falls almost completely silent on the implications of reproductive cloning for the structure of the family.

Increasing the Number of Single-Parent Families

Surely at least some members of the president's council could see those implications. They are hardly obscure. Cloning to produce children has the potential to undermine marriage and the family by enabling unmarried women and men to have children, without the assistance of a second parent.

Given the cultural background, many unmarried individuals will be tempted to clone.

Of course, a single women can have a child now, but not without facing some human complications. A woman can go to a sperm bank, but that means discomfort over the father's anonymity. More often, a Murphy Brown [title character of CBS sitcom that aired from 1988 to 1998, who sparked heated national debate on the importance of two-parent homes when she had a child out of wedlock in the 1991–92 season] will have her child by a man she knows. She will get pregnant by him secretly, or on condition that he will decline to press his rights as a father. But cloning will liberate human vanity to allow at least some among us to produce a child wholly in their own image, and thus free of any legal or emotional complications related to the existence of a second parent.

Perhaps this narcissistic impulse will be limited to a few individuals, but I think it would be foolish to bet on that outcome. Humans have a deep drive to reproduce, and a technology that offers both the possibility of a kind of genetic immortality and no-strings-to-a-partner parenthood will almost certainly find a large market once the initial fear factor wears off. America, after all, is the home of individualism. That is both our glory and our danger. Given the cultural background, many unmarried individuals will be tempted to clone.

If that is true, reproductive cloning will spur a substantial increase in single parenting, a practice that few on the Left or the Right would encourage. A new surge in the number of single parents can only further erode the already-weakened institution of marriage. With the rise of clone single parenthood, the social sanction against bearing a child out of wedlock will be further dampened, even for natural parents.

Advocates of innovations like reproductive cloning often dismiss even secular arguments about the importance of the traditional family. . .as somehow secretly religious.

An Institution Worth Protecting

These are the fairly obvious social consequences of cloning to produce children. Why does the report of the President's Council on Bioethics fail to mention them? I think the reason is political. Apparently, the commission is eager to separate the cloning debate from our contentious culture war over the family. And the commission probably fears that linking an attack on cloning with a defense of the traditional family will be dismissed as a covertly religious argument. If all this is true, then I think the commission may have made a serious political error. More deeply, I think the relationship between the cloning debate and our other contentious culture-war issues— and the relationship between all these issues and religion—is in need of clarification.

Let me first acknowledge that *Human Cloning and Human Dignity* does contain a discussion of the negative effects of reproductive cloning on the family and society. Yet even that discussion is framed almost entirely in terms of the psychology of cloning—of its tendency to undermine individual autonomy, identity, and dignity. What's missing is a disciplined attempt to foresee the effects that cloning can be expected to have on both the rate of single parenthood, and the prevalence of marriage.

Consider the costs of failing to mention the real social effects of cloning. Right now, the common knock on the council's report is that it doesn't make an actual argument against reproductive cloning. The commission, and especially its chairman, Leon Kass, stress cloning's affront to human dignity, thereby putting their trust in "the wisdom of repugnance." That is, Kass and the commission argue that our felt distaste for cloning is an intimation of the truth about the practice's intolerable affront to our humanity. Advocates of cloning dismiss the "wisdom of repugnance" idea as mumbo jumbo. As any defender of liberty knows, mere discomfort does not constitute a legitimate or rational reason to restrict someone else's freedom. In America, without evidence or argument about real social harm, there is no legal or political basis for restricting anything. So by refusing to highlight cloning's inevitable tendency to increase the rate of single parenthood, the commission has stripped itself of the only sort of argument that has legal or political traction. True, in the matter of cloning we are dealing not simply with the rights of free adults, but with the fate of helpless children. Yet that only makes it more urgent to point to specific social harms.

Not that the Kass commission's arguments about human dignity and the wisdom of repugnance actually *are* mumbo jumbo. On the contrary, they are vitally important and deeply true. But we cannot fully understand *why* they are true until we see how inseparable the issues of dignity and repugnance are from the social effects of cloning. Our feelings of repugnance at unconventional practices are warning signs. Taboos are essentially signals that a social institution is under threat. It is true that repugnance, in and of itself, cannot serve as proof that a given institution ought to be protected. There was a time when the thought of interracial marriage was deeply disgusting. Nonetheless, segregation was not an institution worth protecting. Stable two-parent families, on the other hand, are worth protecting. Part of our repulsion at the idea of cloning is a signal that asexual reproduction puts the two-parent family in jeopardy.

I cannot think of a greater threat to all that the public still values in the traditional ethos of marriage and family than reproductive cloning.

The Religious and Secular Perspectives

But what about the claim that a defense of the traditional family is merely a religious argument in disguise, and therefore inappropriate for use in the public sphere? To answer that question we need a conception of what a religion is. One way to think about religion is to see it as a system of approbation and repugnance that serves to protect the central institutions of a given society. This same point can be framed in two different kinds of language, either religious or secular. (And either approach, or even both, could be true.) On the one hand, you can believe that God has revealed that which is praiseworthy and that which is abominable, so as to keep his people righteous and holy. On the other hand, you can believe that religion's practices and prohibitions have come into being as a way of protecting society's essential institutions. Despite the difference in language and perspective, each of these beliefs is actually making the same basic sociological point.

Let me be clear. Arguments about what God has or hasn't decreed cannot sway, and should not sway, non-believers. Yet advocates of innovations like reproductive cloning often dismiss even secular arguments about the importance of the traditional family, or human dignity, as somehow secretly religious. Supposedly, the mere resemblance of these secular arguments to religious injunctions proves that the arguments are invalid for all non-believers. That is nonsense. A thoughtful skeptic would see the matter in reverse. If religious folk believe that God has forbidden a particular practice, then they must believe it because that practice really does undermine a critical social function. Religion itself is a social institution. So if you're truly a skeptic, you need to provide a secular explanation of why a given society's religious beliefs have taken a particular form in the first place.

Discomfort Signals Serious Social Costs

When the pope says that any sexual relations not directed toward reproduction within the context of marriage tend to threaten the structure of the traditional family, he is absolutely right. It is not necessary to be Catholic—or religious—to grant the acuity of the pope's sociological insight. In fact, it is not even necessary to agree with the pope about the need to forbid non-reproductive and non-marital sexual relations to see the validity of the connection he is making. The truth is, a whole series of non-marital or non-reproductive practices that have gained social approval over the last thirty years—from birth control, to abortion, to premarital sex, to homosexuality—have in fact helped to undermine the structure of the traditional family. That is true, whether or not you are religious, and whether you think these developments have been positive or not.

There are three basic reactions to the sociological truths about the family and sexuality uttered by the pope. (Since I myself am neither Catholic nor religious, I will describe the three reactions in secular language. Yet the same points could be made in religious terms.) On the one hand, the feeling of distaste for sexual-reproductive practices that undermine the traditional family can remain wholly in place, as it does for the traditionally religious. On the other hand, the social taboo on these practices can collapse almost completely, as it has for some libertarians, and for some radical gay thinkers as well. But it is also possible for the taboo on non-traditional sexual and reproductive practices to weaken, yet remain partially in place, as it has for many (maybe most) Americans.

Every time some proposed sexual-reproductive innovation arouses our discomfort or distaste, it is a sign that yet another support beam is about to be pulled out from the structure of the traditional family. Nonetheless, for the middle group, in whom the old taboos are present, yet no longer fully in place, the mere feeling of repugnance cannot, by itself, decide the issue. But that feeling of discomfort can serve as a signal that there are real social costs to the change in question—costs that must be weighed against the benefits. From this "middle ground" frame of reference, it is entirely possible to decide that, say, birth control is worth what it costs in family stability, while reproductive cloning is not.

Yet by confining itself to repugnance alone—by declining to connect the feelings of indignity that cloning arouses with the concrete and calculable social harms that these feelings point to—the President's Council on Bioethics has short-circuited its own argument, thereby rendering informed prudential calculation impossible.

Benefitting Only a Few Members of Society

Getting down to cases, the omission of the single-parenting issue leaves cloning opponents vulnerable to emotionally pow-

erful arguments made by, say, parents who want to clone because one of them is carrying a debilitating genetic disease, or
a grieving couple who want to replace a dead child. The goods
at stake in such cases are real, if far from unmixed. (Why burden a child with the sense that he has to replicate his dead
sibling?) Yet these goods are also exceedingly rare. Isolated advantages like this are easily overbalanced by the larger harm to
society as a whole from an upsurge in single parenting. But to
show this, family structure needs to be invoked.

Given the very real difficulties of linking the cloning debate to our culture war over the family, I cannot deny that the
commission may be right to avoid the single-parent issue. Yet
in the years since the Murphy Brown flap, things have changed.
Ever since Barbara Dafoe Whitehead's famous "Dan Quayle
Was Right" article [which praised Dan Quayle's speech criti-
cizing Murphy Brown's decision to raise her child as a single
mother], a rough consensus has emerged, on both sides of the
political aisle, that marriage really does have advantages over
single parenthood. Reproductive cloning, by actually encouraging single parenthood on a mass scale, flies directly in the
face of that consensus. I cannot think of a greater threat to all
that the public still values in the traditional ethos of marriage
and family than reproductive cloning.

Maybe, even without telling the whole truth about the
harm that reproductive cloning will work upon the family, the
President's Commission on Bioethics will be able to obtain a
ban. On the other hand, maybe it won't. In any case, if the
safety issues are resolved, the debate will flare again. . . .

Here, then, is the more complete argument: You don't
have to be religious, or even very conservative, to recognize
that two parents raising a child are better than one. Reproductive cloning will encourage a major expansion of single-parent
families, while offering (very mixed) benefits to only a small
percentage of traditional couples. In short, cloning to produce
children is a dangerous idea.

9

Cloning Animals for Food Is Morally Permissible

Sigrid Fry-Revere

Sigrid Fry-Revere is the former director of bioethics studies at the Cato Institute, a libertarian public-policy organization. She has published several articles in academic journals such as the Cambridge Quarterly of Healthcare Ethics, *the* Journal of Clinical Ethics *and the* American Journal of Bioethics. *Her areas of study include genetic engineering, reproductive technologies, and end-of-life decision making.*

Cloning is a new technology that helps farmers and livestock breeders do what they have been doing for thousands of years— manipulating breeds to produce animals with desirable traits. Because this manipulation does not affect the quality of the food produced by these cloned animals, the government should not impose regulation on the industry. Instead, the morality of individual breeders and consumers should dictate how cloning is utilized in breeding and how its foodstuffs are received in the marketplace.

[In December 2006,] the FDA's [Food and Drug Administration's] Center for Veterinary Medicine ... issued three documents related to cloned foods:

- "Animal Cloning: A Draft Risk Assessment"

- "Animal Cloning: Proposed Risk Management Plan for Clones and Their Progeny"

Sigrid Fry-Revere, "Cloned Food 101," *Cato at Liberty*, December 29, 2006. Republished with permission of CATO, conveyed through Copyright Clearance Center, Inc.

- "Guideline No. 179: Guidance for Industry Use of Edible Products from Animal Clones or Their Progeny for Human Food or Animal Feed". . .

The FDA concluded that, while there were little data, the data available indicated that "SCNT [somatic cell nuclear transfer, i.e., cloning] results in an increased frequency of health risks to animals involved in the cloning process, but these do not differ qualitatively from those observed in other ARTs [assisted reproductive technologies] or natural breeding." Furthermore, "[e]xtensive evaluation of the available data has not identified any food consumption risks or subtle hazards in healthy clones of cattle, swine, or goats."

The FDA has asked for a "voluntary" moratorium [on cloned food] because, under current law, the agency probably doesn't have the authority to ban foods made from clones.

In short, unless [public and professional] comments [on the documents] indicate otherwise, food from cloned animals will be on the market [sometime in late 2007] and require no additional labeling to distinguish it from food products from non-cloned animals.

Avoiding Misunderstandings About Cloned Livestock

Most objections to "cloned foods" stem from a misunderstanding of the technology and its ramifications.First, not the food, but the animal used to produce the food is what is cloned. Potentially, the actual clone could be used as food but, since it costs $15,000 to $20,000 to produce a clone, it is usually only the clone's milk or offspring that are intended for the food market.

Cloning is not a form of genetic engineering. The DNA provided by the animal being cloned is not altered. Cloning is a form of assisted reproduction that creates an identical twin at a later time. Any accidental alteration of the DNA results in death of the clone usually in the lab, but occasionally one survives through gestation and birth, but not beyond the perinatal period. Thus, all clones that have the potential of entering the food supply or of being bred are genetically identical to the animal that was cloned.

Food from cloned animals simply does not differ from regular food in any manner that justifies regulation under the FFDCA.

Food from clones poses no more risk to the consumer than the animal being cloned. The susceptibility to disease or other conditions that may disqualify clones from food production is no greater than that of the original animal. Thus, the fact that an animal is a clone poses no unique risk to the food supply.

The first sheep (Dolly) was cloned in 1996. The first cow was cloned in 1998 and the first pig in 2000.

In 2001, the FDA decided to study the issue of food from cloned animals and asked the food industry not to introduce any food produced by clones or their progeny into the market. The FDA's notice of publication that accompanies the afore-mentioned drafts requests that this "voluntary moratorium" continue.

It is possible that some cloned animals or their progeny have already entered the food supply, but there is no definitive evidence that this has happened.

The FDA has asked for a "voluntary" moratorium because, under current law, the agency probably doesn't have the authority to ban foods made from clones. Unless Congress amends the Federal Food, Drug, and Cosmetic Act (FFDCA), this will continue to be the case regardless of what the FDA decides when it publishes its final rule.

The milk and beef from cloned cows is indistinguishable from that produced by other cows. It's not adulterated; there are no additives. The following is an oversimplified description of federal law, but should shed some light on why the FDA is proceeding as it is. Basically, federal law (the FFDCA) presumes that unadulterated food is safe. The FDA has the authority to regulate the use of additives and to require accuracy in labeling. Labeling may be regulated to assure that the identity of the food is correctly represented (margarine is not butter) and that potentially harmful additives or allergens are indicated on the label. Food from cloned animals simply does not differ from regular food in any manner that justifies regulation under the FFDCA.

While . . . concerns [about cloning] hold legitimate moral sway with various portions of the population, they are not grounds for government action.

It is time to give some clarification regarding the phrase "genetic engineering." Genetically engineered animals have been genetically altered, not just reproduced. Under a broad definition of "genetic engineering," all animal husbandry that involves changing the genetic makeup from one generation to the next involves genetic engineering. In this sense, each time a breeder chooses a mate for an animal, he is engaged in genetic engineering. This type of genetic engineering actually takes place through selective reproduction. A newer type of genetic engineering, which is what most people mean when they use the term, refers to genetic alterations made by man not through selective breeding but through selecting the actual specific genes that will be combined. This can also involve taking out or adding genetic material, including the addition of genetic materials from different breeds, species, phyla, or even kingdoms. The resulting animal or plant is called "transgenic" if foreign DNA is integrated into the genome.

There are over a billion acres of land, most of it in the United States, planted with strains of transgenic crops. These crops, for the most part, are corn, soybeans and cotton.

At this time, there is only one transgenic fish approved for sale in the United States, and it is an aquarium fish, not for human consumption. There is, however, a petition pending with the FDA to approve a transgenic salmon, and it will be labeled as such if it is approved.

The Center for Food Safety and several other consumer groups have filed a Citizen Petition with the FDA encouraging the agency to regulate cloned foods as new animal drugs. Under the FFDCA, drugs require pre-approval for safety and efficacy before being marketed. This is quite a stretch. The relevant part of the FFDCA definition of a "drug" according to the petition is "any articles (other than food) intended to affect the structure or any function of the body of man or other animals." It is further worth noting that genetically modified foods, including transgenic animals, require pre-market approval by the FDA because they are considered as containing "food additives." This actually makes some definitional sense since genetic material is added or changed to create a genetically modified plant or animal. But, this same logic does not hold for cloning.

The Government Should Not Regulate Cloned Food

The conclusion I draw from these facts is that the FDA should not be involved at all in regulating food from clones or their progeny. Under existing law, the FDA doesn't have the authority to regulate food from clones even if there were a safety issue.

Regarding labeling—that issue will take care of itself without FDA interference. If there is enough public concern that food produced from clones or their progeny is unsafe, then producers of organic foods will start specifying "Not from cloned animals" on their labels in the same way they have advertised "Not from animals treated with hormones or antibiotics."

The Center for Food Safety claims that "63% of Americans would not buy cloned food, even if FDA deemed the products safe." They present these data from a 2005 poll as an argument for regulation. I think such poll results only justify purchasing stock in organic food companies that promise not to sell products from cloned animals—but not government intervention.

Morality Is an Individual's Concern

The ethical concerns addressed here are primarily moral considerations that legitimately could influence actions taken by individual breeders, producers, and consumers, but not legitimately be used to argue for government intervention. Even the FDA agrees with this point. In its proposed risk management plan, the agency states: "The Draft Risk Assessment is strictly a science-based evaluation of animal health and food consumption risks, and the Proposed Risk Management Plan and Draft Guidance for Industry do not address any ethical or other non-science based concerns regarding animal cloning."

Most ethical objections to cloning and genetic engineering in general come from a fear of the unknown consequences of such technology, a religious or moral objection to tampering with natural reproduction, and/or a concern for preventing cruelty to animals. While all these concerns hold legitimate moral sway with various portions of the population, they are not grounds for government action. We live in a pluralist society and those who disagree on religious or moral grounds with cloning should be free to speak out, boycott, or not participate in the objectionable activity, but those who do not object should be equally free to participate in producing food from clones and/or eating it.

The one legitimate concern I see with cloning is one almost as old as animal husbandry itself. By its very nature, manipulating a gene pool to create certain desired phenotypes creates a homogeneity that can put the whole group at risk. As a 25-year veteran breeder of rare-breed dogs and cats, I know first-hand that breeders often attempt to ferment type at the expense of health. A lack of genetic diversity in purebred animals caused by too much inbreeding makes those animals more susceptible to disease, shorter-lived, and more prone to unhealthy offspring. Domestically bred animals lose their genetic resilience when intentional line-breeding or the overuse of certain choice animals makes it difficult to find animals that aren't related.

To prevent such homogeneity, some breeders feel it is their moral obligation not to flood the gene pool with one particular genotype. They do this by not breeding two animals related more closely than five generations back or by not breeding their pride stud more than four times a year. Such ethical standards are usually set by individual breeders or private breed associations. Cloning itself is not inbreeding but it can result in flooding a gene pool; for example, there are reports of a farmer who has cloned his prize bull five times already. Now an animal whose genetic material would appear in X number of offspring, will in fact appear in X^6 number of offspring. In this way, cloning can over-saturate a gene pool with a particular animal's genes, making the group more susceptible to intentional or accidental inbreeding and, in turn, genetically weaken the group as a whole.

Advantages of Cloning

Like cloning, genetic engineering could be used to create consistency within a breed, but it also could be used to create diversity. Genetic engineering could help eliminate genetically linked diseases, even those in rather homogeneous groups. It could also be used to create more diversity in ways that help preserve the desired traits without creating too much homogeneity.

Also, while individual breeds within a species become more homogeneous, genetic engineering could help the number of breeds proliferate—just look at the number of dog, cat, and bovine breeds that exist today. It certainly would be disappointing for those who like the taste of a particular kind of beef to learn that the breed of cattle that produces that beef is failing in part because of too much cloning, but that would not mean the end of all beef or all bovines. It would simply mean regenerating the breed either from a survivor, hopefully genetically engineering out the flaw that caused problems, or altering another breed to have the characteristics that were prized in the breed that failed.

None of the ethical issues presented by cloning food-producing animals are new. Cloning and genetic engineering only provide new and more effective methods of doing what humans have been doing for millennia—that is, manipulating the genetic makeup of plants and animals to create better food. Put another way, humans have been tampering with nature, playing God with the creation of animals, and eating their creations for thousands of years. The only thing that has changed is the technology. The goals and the ethical problems inherent in those goals remain the same. And, as is usually the case, the very technology that poses potential problems, undoubtedly also holds the solution to those problems should they arise.

10

Cloning Animals for Food Is Morally Impermissible

Nina Mak

Nina Mak is a research analyst for the American Anti-Vivisection Society, a nonprofit animal advocacy and welfare organization that seeks to end experimentation and testing on animals.

Cloning livestock for breeding and food is ethically questionable. Many cloned newborns suffer abnormalities at alarming rates, and the very few cloned animals that survive to adulthood also commonly experience health problems. Such animal welfare concerns cannot be ignored when debating the application of cloning science. If cloning livestock is to continue, the government should at least require that products from these animals be labeled if not otherwise regulated.

The decision to allow or prohibit the cloning of animals for food is far more consequential than most people realize. Yet the Food and Drug Administration (FDA) chose to announce its decision to give a preliminary go-ahead to animal cloning on December 28, 2000, a time of year when most news is likely to be overlooked by a preoccupied public. In addition, while many people are looking for accurate, reliable information about animal cloning in an attempt to understand this ethically-challenging technology, the FDA and the biotech industry have been misrepresenting the facts and confusing the debate.

Nina Mak, "Out of the Lab and into Our Grocery Store? The Problems with Cloning Animals for Food," *AV Magazine*, vol. cxv, Spring 2007, pp. 2–5. Reproduced by permission.

As part of our campaign to end animal cloning, AAVS [American Anti-Vivisection Society] aims to bring clarity to these issues, as well as highlight a serious problem that has generally been overlooked in the discussions on cloning: animal welfare. Cloning need not be too complicated to understand. In fact, the overall message from all the scientific studies on cloning is remarkably clear: cloning is inefficient and unpredictable, resulting in premature death or severe health problems for more than 95 percent of the animals involved. In response, AAVS has launched its End Animal Cloning campaign to prevent the needless animal suffering that cloning causes and to inform the public about the cruel effects of this experimental technology.

Abnormal fetal development is common in clones, which translates into abnormal pregnancies with a host of complications.

Cloning is the term commonly used to refer to a procedure known as somatic cell nuclear transfer (SCNT), the procedure which was first used to create Dolly the sheep in 1996. In SCNT, the genetic material (DNA) of an egg is replaced with the DNA from a donor animal, and the egg is then stimulated to develop into a nearly identical copy of the donor. Since Dolly, researchers have cloned a number of different animals, including cows, pigs, goats, horses, mice, cats, and dogs. The process is far from perfected, however, with only 1–4 percent of cloning attempts succeeding.

Cloning for Breeding Purposes

Agriculture researchers are currently interested in cloning livestock primarily for breeding purposes, in an attempt to create copies of 'valuable' animals. Farmers commonly use the animals who have the best genetics for some desired quality such as fast growth, leaner meat, or high milk production as breeding animals to produce offspring who will have similar qualities. By cloning these 'top' breeders, farmers are trying to extend their reproductive potential and create whole herds or flocks with these uniform characteristics.

However, cloning highly productive animals exacerbates animal welfare concerns, because these animals tend to suffer from painful infections of the udder, lameness, and other 'production-related' diseases. In addition, cloning raises concerns about genetic diversity, because herds of identical animals are more susceptible to disease outbreaks. Overall, cloning requires a significantly greater level of involvement and interference with animals' reproductive performance than conventional production methods, which raises unprecedented concerns and ethical challenges that fly in the face of the public's interest in animal welfare and humane treatment of farm animals.

Even the few cloned animals who live for longer than 6 months and appear otherwise healthy have been known to suffer unexpected health consequences later in life.

Perhaps even more important, cloning is also used to produce copies of transgenic animals. Transgenic animals are those who most likely have been engineered with genes from another species for any of a variety of purposes: to have better traits for production (such as faster growth, disease resistance, altered milk or meat products with 'health benefits' for humans, etc.); to produce pharmaceuticals in their milk, blood, urine, or semen (pharming); or to produce tissues and organs for transplantation into humans (xenotransplantation). If animal cloning is approved, the generation and proliferation of transgenic animals are likely to become major applications of cloning technology. Clearly, such implications raise numerous troubling ethical questions, which cannot be ignored in the decision-making process on cloning.

Threats to Animal Health and Welfare

The remarkable inefficiency of cloning poses immediate threats to animal welfare. Fewer than one percent of cloning attempts will result in a successful birth, and of those who are born, only a relatively small percentage are healthy enough to live for more than a few days or weeks. With such low success rates, not only do the cloned animals endure suffering, but so do hundreds of additional animals as they are pumped with hormones and their eggs harvested, or as they are implanted with embryos, often repeatedly, in an attempt to produce just one cloned animal who survives.

With such obvious and overwhelming health problems routinely reported in cloned animals, it is clear that cloning seriously threatens animal well-being.

According to the FDA's ... analysis of animal cloning risks, abnormal fetal development is common in clones, which translates into abnormal pregnancies with a host of complications that threaten the lives of the unborn clones and their surrogate mothers. For example, a typically fatal condition known as hydrops, in which the mother and/or the fetus swells with fluid, occurs frequently in clone pregnancies. From the data presented by the FDA, hydrops has occurred in 28 percent of clone pregnancies, with one study (conducted by Cyagra, a biotech company leading the push for cloned foods) reporting hydrops in over 50 percent of cases. In contrast, hydrops occurs rarely or never in pregnancies produced through artificial insemination or natural breeding.

Clone pregnancies are also associated with a greater risk of late term loss, with roughly 45 percent of pregnancies reported lost in the second or third trimester in studies at a research farm in France. Such losses, normally uncommon in conventional pregnancies, "expose the recipients [surrogates] to conditions that threaten their welfare."

Based on published data and the FDA's own report, it is clear that abnormalities are also the norm, not the exception, for the few cloned animals who survive birth. Cloned animals suffer from respiratory distress; hypoglycemia; weakened immune systems; developmental problems; deformities; malformed livers, kidneys, or hearts; and a variety of ailments that claim the lives of approximately one-third of neonates (newborns).

Many of these ailments are related to Large Offspring Syndrome (LOS), a commonly observed problem with cloned animals in which the animal develops to be significantly bigger at birth than a conventional animal. It is not uncommon for the animal to be twice the normal size, and in one study, a lamb was reported as being five times larger than normal. In fact, LOS occurred in over 50 percent of calf clones included in the FDA's report, compared to 6 percent of conventionally bred animals.

In addition, according to a recent study conducted by Cyagra, 75 percent of cloned calves required antibiotics, and almost half of the cloned animals who survived birth died within the first five months, despite access to extensive veterinary care, and despite the fact that any of more than 10 different interventions were performed.

Even the few cloned animals who live for longer than 6 months and appear otherwise healthy have been known to suffer unexpected health consequences later in life. Studies in cows, for example, have documented cases of sudden, unexplained deaths and subclinical pathologies that had gone undetected. In fact, in an article ... published in *The New England Journal of Medicine*, Rudolf Jaenisch, a prominent MIT [Massachusetts Institute of Technology] cloning researcher, stated that "given the available evidence, it may be exceedingly difficult, if not impossible, to generate healthy cloned animals. . . ."

Informing the Public

With such obvious and overwhelming health problems routinely reported in cloned animals, it is clear that cloning seriously threatens animal well-being. While the FDA chooses to deflect focus from this fact, skirting the issue by avoiding discussion on the tremendous frequency with which these problems occur, AAVS is actively working to inform the public about these hidden costs of cloning.

Clearly, questions about the impact of cloning on animal welfare have yet to be adequately addressed, much less resolved. This is despite the fact that 63 percent of Americans want the government to factor in ethical considerations when making a decision on animal cloning. As a result, AAVS has petitioned the FDA and is working with Congress, in conjunction with the Center for Food Safety and numerous other consumer, animal advocacy, and environmental organizations, to establish a forum for the public discussion of these issues, and to instate a mandatory moratorium on the sale of cloned foods in the meantime.

In addition, AAVS is monitoring and supporting legislative efforts to require that cloned foods, if they are approved for sale be labeled as such. Labels are important to help consumers make informed decisions about their food purchases, especially the majority of Americans, who have ethical, religious, or safety concerns about cloning and want to avoid cloned foods.

Cloning is remarkably inefficient and unpredictable yet also highly consequential. The FDA should not allow cloning to proceed without any regulations and concern for the welfare of the animals involved.

Organizations to Contact

The editors have compiled the following list of organizations concerned with the issues debated in this book. The descriptions are derived from materials provided by the organizations. All have publications or information available for interested readers. The list was compiled on the date of publication of the present volume; the information provided here may change. Be aware that many organizations take several weeks or longer to respond to inquiries, so allow as much time as possible.

Americans to Ban Cloning (ABC)
1100 H Street, NW, Suite 700, Washington, DC   20005
(202) 347-6840 • fax: (202) 347-6849
Web site: www.cloninginformation.org

Based in the United States, ABC seeks a comprehensive, global ban on human cloning. The organization's Web site provides links to current new articles, commentary, and testimony about issues related to the cloning debate and provides instructions on how concerned individuals can contact their government representatives to encourage support of a ban on cloning.

American Veterinary Medical Association (AVMA)
1931 North Meacham Road, Suite 100
Schaumburg, IL   60173-4360
(847) 925-8070 • fax: (847) 925-1329
e-mail: avmainfo@avma.org
Web site: www.avma.org

AVMA is a nonprofit organization that represents veterinarians working in any capacity. Its mission is to further the veterinary medicine profession to the benefit of both animals and humans. While the AVMA does not take an official position on the cloning of animals, in June 2005 its executive board did put forth a policy on the Creation and Use of Genetically Modified Animals that allows for genetic research on animals as long as the research "does not impact the integrity of the environment and the general health and well being of genetically modified animals remains preferential to human values and needs." Issues related to cloning have been addressed in the bimonthly *Journal of the American Veterinary Medical Association* and the monthly publication *American Journal of Veterinary Research.*

The Center for Bioethics and Human Dignity (CBHD)
Trinity International University, 2065 Half Day Road
Deerfield, IL   60015
(847) 317-8180 • fax: (847) 317-8101
e-mail: info@cbhd.org
Web site: www.cbhd.org

CBHD works to assess the bioethical nature of scientific advances from a Christian perspective. The organization focuses on issues such as biotechnology, death and dying, genetics, reproductive ethics, and cloning. The CBHD position statement on cloning calls for a comprehensive ban on reproductive and therapeutic cloning, stating that the publically opposed practice of human reproductive cloning threatens human dignity, and cloning embryos for inevitable destruction in research or medical therapies is inconsistent with U.S. legal tradition. Articles and commentary written by CBHD scholars as well as others with similar viewpoints can be read on the center's Web site.

Center for Food Safety (CFS)
660 Pennsylvania Avenue, SE, #302, Washington, DC   20003
(202) 547-9359 • fax: (202) 547-9429
e-mail: office@centerforfoodsafety.org
Web site: www.centerforfoodsafety.org

Founded by the International Center for Technology Assessment in 1997, CFS analyzes the usefulness of new technologies and alternative methods in providing sustainable food sources.

CFS seeks to educate the public through its educational materials and influence policy by suggesting guidelines for policy makers. The center adamantly opposes the use of cloned animals in food production. Reports on animal cloning for food can be read on CFS's Web site.

Council for Responsible Genetics (CRG)
5 Upland Road, Suite 3, Cambridge, MA   02140
(617) 868-0870 • fax: (617) 491-5344
e-mail: crg@gene-watch.org
Web site: www.gene-watch.org

CRG seeks to educate and engage the public in issues relating to current and emerging biotechnologies. Focuses of the organization include genetic determinism, cloning and human genetic manipulation, and women and biotechnology. The CRG opposes human reproductive cloning and encourages international debate as to the moral and regulatory constraints that should be imposed on this technology. *Gene Watch* is the bimonthly publication of the organization.

Do No Harm: The Coalition of Americans for Research Ethics
1100 H Street, NW, Suite 700, Washington, DC   20005
(202) 347-6840 • fax: (202) 347-6849
Web site: www.stemcellresearch.org

Do No Harm was founded to provide a voice of opposition to embryonic stem cell research. The organization opposes stem cell research and therapy that results in the destruction of a human embryo, whether that embryo was the result of in vitro fertilization, cloning, or some other method of uniting a sperm and egg. Do No Harm has called for a ban on therapeutic cloning. Commentary, fact sheets, and testimony promoting this ban can be read on the organization's Web site.

The Human Cloning Foundation (HCF)
e-mail: contactus@humancloning.org
Web site: www.humancloning.org

HCF was founded in 1998 to provide a supportive voice to the human cloning, stem cell research, and biotechnology debates. The heart of the foundation is its Web site, which provides a searchable clearinghouse of articles promoting human cloning, both reproductive and therapeutic, and touting its benefits.

Institute on Biotechnology and the Human Future
565 West Adams Street, Chicago, IL   60661
(312) 906-5337
e-mail: info@thehumanfuture.org
Web site: www.thehumanfuture.org

The Institute on Biotechnology and the Human Future examines current and emerging advances in biotechnology from a cultural and ethical perspective and seeks to encourage those technologies and policies that promote human life and progress. Generally, the organization's background material views cloning skeptically and questions the value of this technology. The institute's Web site provides impact and policy background information on human cloning as well as commentary from institute scholars assessing the value and cost of both reproductive and therapeutic cloning.

Institute for Ethics and Emerging Technologies (IEET)
Williams 229B, Trinity College, 300 Summit Street
Hartford, CT   06106
(860) 297-2376
e-mail: director@ieet.org
Web site: www.ieet.org

Founded in 2004 by a philosopher and a bioethicist, IEET seeks to provide a forum for individuals to debate the most responsible and constructive ways to deal with human enhancement technologies. While acknowledging that these technologies can and should be used to help better human life, IEET is careful to recognize the importance of examining the ethical and societal implications of these technologies' use. Scholars from the IEET argue that both reproductive and therapeutic cloning should be developed and allowed for use by all individuals. The *Journal of Evolution and Technology* is the quarterly, electronic publication of the institute.

International Bioethics Committee (IBC)

2 United Nations Plaza, Room 900, New York, NY   10017
(212) 963-5995 • fax: (212) 963-8014
e-mail: newyork@unesco.org
Web site: www.unesco.org/ibc

The IBC is the committee within the United Nations Educational, Scientific and Cultural Organization charged with ensuring that human dignity and freedom are observed as advances in biotechnology continue worldwide. Declarations laying out guidelines include the *Universal Declaration on the Human Genome and Human Rights*, the *International Declaration on Human Genetic Data*, and the *Universal Declaration on Bioethics and Human Rights*. These and other publications can be accessed online.

International Center for Technology Assessment (CTA)

660 Pennsylvania Ave. SE, Suite 302, Washington, DC   20003
(202) 547-9359
e-mail: info@icta.org
Web site: www.icta.org

CTA seeks to educate the public about the economic, ethical, social, environmental, and political impacts resulting from the use of emerging biotechnologies. Among others, the CTA investigates nanotechnology, human biotechnology, and global warming. With regards to cloning, the CTA worries that the use of this technology will place undue emphasis on the relationship between one's genetic traits and their abilities. As a result, the CTA advocates strong regulations to control the widespread use and proliferation of this and other human biotechnologies. Reports from the center can be read online.

Nuffield Council on Bioethics
Communications and External Affairs Manager
28 Bedford Square   WC1B 3JS
  London
(44) (020) 7681 9619 • fax: (44) (020) 7637 1712
e-mail: bioethics@nuffieldbioethics.org
Web site: www.nuffieldbioethics.org

The Nuffield Council on Bioethics was established in 1991 to identify and assess ethical concerns resulting from the advances of biotechnology. The council encourages the public to become involved in the debate on technologies such as cloning and stem cell research through the distribution of educational materials. Papers published by the organization can be accessed online.

President's Council on Bioethics
1425 New York Avenue, NW, Suite C100
Washington, DC   20005
(202) 296-4669
e-mail: info@bioethics.gov
Web site: www.bioethics.gov

The President's Council on Bioethics was created by executive order in November 2001 by President George W. Bush. The council's mission is to provide advice to the president when bioethical issues arise as biomedical science and technology continue to advance. In addition, the council is charged with providing a forum for balanced debate about issues such as cloning and stem cell research and their impact on society. In its existence thus far, the council has published numerous reports, including *Human Dignity and Bioethics: Essays Commissioned by the President's Council on Bioethics* and *Human Cloning and Human Dignity: An Ethical Inquiry*. These reports and others can be read online.

Reproductive Cloning Network
506 Hudson Street, New York, NY   10014
(212) 255-1439

Web site: www.reproductivecloning.net

The Reproductive Cloning Network provides a database of articles exploring the scientific basis of reproductive cloning. Additionally, links to other sites and companies involved with reproductive cloning are available on the organization's Web site. This network is affiliated with the Human Cloning Foundation, which examines the moral and ethical debate about cloning.

World Transhumanist Association (WTA)
P.O. Box 128, Willington, CT   06279
e-mail: secretary@transhumanism.org
Web site: www.transhumanism.org

WTA seeks to advance the ethical use of technology to further human capabilities. The organization advocates for technological developments that it believes will help humans to live better lives. In accordance with these ideas, the WTA supports continued research into human and animal cloning, and states that if found to be safe and effective, humans should have the option to utilize this technology for both reproductive and therapeutic purposes. Articles about cloning and other technological advances supported by the WTA can be read on its Web site.

Bibliography

Books

Michael Bellomo   *The Stem Cell Divide: The Facts, the Fiction, and the Fear Driving the Greatest Scientific, Political, and Religious Debate of Our Time.* New York: American Management Association, 2006.

Andrea L. Bonnicksen   *Crafting a Cloning Policy: From Dolly to Stem Cells.* Washington, DC: Georgetown University Press, 2002.

Michael C. Brannigan, ed.   *Ethical Issues in Human Cloning: Cross-disciplinary Perspectives.* New York: Seven Bridges, 2001.

Eric Cohen   *In the Shadow of Progress: Being Human in the Age of Technology.* New York: Encounter, 2008.

Ronald Cole-Turner, ed.   *Beyond Cloning: Religion and the Remaking of Humanity.* Harrisburg, PA: Trinity, 2001.

Brendan Curran   *A Terrible Beauty Is Born: Clones, Genes and the Future of Mankind.* New York: Taylor and Francis, 2003.

Stephen D. Fairbanks, ed.   *Cloning: Chronology, Abstracts and Guide to Books.* New York: Nova Science, 2004.

Sarah Franklin   *Dolly Mixtures: The Remaking of Genealogy.* Durham, NC: Duke University Press, 2007.

Francis Fukuyama *Our Posthuman Future: Consequences of the Biotechnology Revolution.* New York: Farrar, Straus and Giroux, 2002.

Leon R. Kass and *The Ethics of Human Cloning.*
James Q. Wilson   Lanham, MD: AEI Press, 1998.

Arlene Judith   *A Clone of Your Own: The Science*
Klotzko   *and Ethics of Cloning.* New York: Cambridge University Press, 2006.

Russell Korobkin   *Stem Cell Century: Law and Policy for a Breakthrough Technology.* New Haven, CT: Yale University Press, 2007.

Stephen E. Levick *Clone Being: Exploring the Psychological and Social Dimensions.* Lanham, MD: Rowman and Littlefield, 2004.

Aaron D. Levine   *Cloning: A Beginner's Guide.* Oxford, England: Oneworld, 2007.

Kerry Lynn   *Illegal Beings: Human Clones and the*
Macintosh   *Law.* New York: Cambridge University Press, 2005.

Jane Maienschein *Whose View of Life? Embryos, Cloning, and Stem Cells.* Cambridge, MA: Harvard University Press, 2003.

Gregory E. Pence   *Cloning After Dolly: Who's Still Afraid?* Lanham, MD: Rowman and Littlefield, 2004.

Gregory E. Pence   *Who's Afraid of Human Cloning.* Lanham, MD: Rowman and Littlefield, 1998.

Mary Warnock   *Making Babies: Is There a Right to Have Children?* New York: Oxford University Press, 2002.

Brent Waters and Ronald Cole-Turner, eds.   *God and the Embryo: Religious Voices on Stem Cells and Cloning.* Washington, DC: Georgetown University Press, 2003.

Ian Wilmut and Roger Highfield   *After Dolly: The Promise and Perils of Human Cloning.* New York: Norton, 2007.

Periodicals

Peter Aldhous and Andy Coghlan   "Ten Years on, Has the Cloning Dream Died?" *New Scientist*, July 1, 2006.

American Spectator   "No, the Stem Cell Debate Is Not Over," April 2008.

Ryan T. Anderson   "The End of the Stem-Cell Wars," *Weekly Standard*, December 3, 2007.

Donald Bruce   "Over-egging the Clones?" *New Scientist*, January 20, 2007.

Andy Coghlan — "Cloned Human Embryo 'May Have Generated Stem Cells,'" *New Scientist*, January 26, 2008.

James Kanter — "Europe's Ethics Panel Says Cloning Harms Animals," *New York Times*, January 18, 2008.

Verlyn Klinkenborg — "Closing the Barn Door After the Cows Have Gotten Out," *New York Times*, January 23, 2008.

Sally Lehrman — "No More Cloning Around," *Scientific American*, August 2008.

Bruno Maddox — "Blinded by Science," *Discover*, November 2006.

Hugh McLachlan — "Comment: Let's Legalise Cloning," *New Scientist*, July 21, 2007.

Henry I. Miller — "Food from Cloned Animals Is Part of Our Brave New World," *Trends in Biotechnology*, May 2007.

Richard Monastersky — "A Second Life for Cloning," *Chronicle of Higher Education*, February 3, 2006.

Richard Monastersky — "Stem-Cell Advances Could Speed Research," *Chronicle of Higher Education*, November 30, 2007.

Neil Munro — "Cloning Critics Split?" *National Journal*, February 2, 2008.

David S. Oderberg — "Human Embryonic Stem Cell Research: What's Wrong with It?" *Human Life Review*, Fall 2005.

David Oderberg and Julian Savulescu — "How Will History Judge Cloning?" *Times Higher Education Supplement,* May 6, 2005.

Sharon Oosthoek — "I'll Have the Cloneburger and Fries," *New Scientist,* April 26, 2008.

Alice Park — "Man Makes Life?" *Time,* February 4, 2008.

Virginia Postrel — "Criminalizing Science?" *Forbes,* October 17, 2005.

Scientific American — "The Beef with Cloned Meat," March 2007.

Wesley J. Smith — "Cloning Doubletalk," The Daily Standard, March 26, 2007. http://www.weeklystandard.com/Content/Public/Articles/000/000/013/441vfewj.asp.

John Tierney — "Are Scientists Playing God? It Depends on Your Religion," *New York Times,* November 20, 2007.

Time — "Is Cloned Meat Safe to Eat?" January 28, 2008.

David Van Gend — "Prometheus, Pandora, and the Myths of Cloning," *Human Life Review,* Summer/Fall 2006.

Pamela R. Winnick — "Misadventures of Cloning," *Weekly Standard,* February 6, 2006.

Index